"Filling a gap in recent ~~l~~ Matera once again bring~~s~~ ~~exe~~getical and homiletical skills to the apostle Paul, specifically to his preaching. Anyone who reads and absorbs this small but significant—and deeply spiritual—book will be a better interpreter of Paul the preacher and a better preacher of the powerful gospel of the cross and resurrection that Paul proclaimed."

—**Michael J. Gorman**, St. Mary's Seminary & University

"Frank Matera has brought a lifelong passion for Paul to this powerful book, directed to all Christian preachers and readers. It is easier to preach on the Gospel stories than on the Pauline gospel. But our preaching will be enriched if we consider carefully why Paul preached, what he preached, and how he preached. The book contains a carefully nuanced presentation of Paul the preacher and the message he preached: the new creation made universally available in and through the death and resurrection of Jesus Christ. Not only does Matera guide all who exercise the ministry of preaching in the Christian church. He also reminds us that we must practice what we preach. Preaching 'is a ministry of living the gospel one proclaims.' This sentiment has long been credited to Francis of Assisi: Preach the gospel at all times. Occasionally you may have to say something."

—**Francis J. Moloney, SDB**, Catholic Theological College, University of Divinity, Melbourne, Victoria, Australia

"In this unique, integrative volume, a distinguished biblical theologian and experienced practitioner of preaching articulates the theology of preaching he discerns in the Pauline corpus, reflecting on why, what, and how Paul preached, thereby clarifying why, what, and how we should preach today. Readers called to the ministry of proclamation will come away with a renewed sense of the vital importance of this lifelong and life-changing task and invaluable food for thought about what it means to preach with integrity in a Pauline manner, from the perspective of Christ's crucifixion and resurrection."

—**Frances Taylor Gench**, Union Presbyterian Seminary

"Frank Matera's latest offering in his long career of cogent and insightful theological and exegetical studies of the New Testament presents Paul's preaching first in its original context, then discusses how it can continue to be effective across time. This volume explores Paul's preaching from the cross through his theology of proclamation. Focusing on the why, what, and how of Paul's preaching, Matera presents comprehensive theses for integrating Paul's gift of preaching into a necessary challenge for incisive and active homiletics today."

—**Sherri Brown**, Creighton University

"Frank Matera is a renowned interpreter of Paul's letters and theology. With this slim volume, he adds to his impressive portfolio by offering an insightful exposition of Paul's theology and practice of preaching, covering all aspects of this significant but overlooked topic. This book should be required reading for all preachers of the Word from any denomination, but it also offers a wider audience a superb summary of Paul's unparalleled proclamation of the gospel of Jesus Christ."

—**Ronald D. Witherup**, PSS, St. Mary's
Seminary & University

Preaching
from the Cross

Preaching from the Cross

PAUL'S THEOLOGY OF PROCLAMATION

Frank J. Matera

Baker Academic
a division of Baker Publishing Group
Grand Rapids, Michigan

© 2025 by Frank J. Matera

Published by Baker Academic
a division of Baker Publishing Group
Grand Rapids, Michigan
BakerAcademic.com

Printed in the United States of America

Library of Congress Cataloging-in-Publication Data
Names: Matera, Frank J., author.
Title: Preaching from the cross : Paul's theology of proclamation / Frank J. Matera.
Description: Grand Rapids, Michigan : Baker Academic, a division of Baker Publishing
    Group, [2025] | Includes bibliographical references and index.
Identifiers: LCCN 2024029072 | ISBN 9781540968197 (paperback) | ISBN
    9781540968661 (casebound) | ISBN 9781493449439 (ebook) | ISBN 9781493449446
    (pdf)
Subjects: LCSH: Paul, the Apostle, Saint—Criticism, interpretation. | Preaching—
    Biblical teaching.
Classification: LCC BS2651 .M384 2025 | DDC 227/.06—dc23/eng/20240814
LC record available at https://lccn.loc.gov/2024029072

Cover painting detail from *Paul Rebukes the Repentant Peter* (1603), Guido Reni / Artvee

25 26 27 28 29 30 31   7 6 5 4 3 2 1

In memoriam
Msgr. David J. Joyce
Rev. Merle L. Lavoie
Msgr. John P. Meier

Faithful friends and devoted
ministers of the word of God

Contents

Preface

Preaching the gospel and studying the Pauline letters have been lifelong passions. And so I have written this small volume to address an important but neglected topic: Paul's theology of preaching and its implications for our preaching today. To be sure, most Pauline theologies address the question of Paul's proclamation of the gospel, but there are very few studies that focus on his preaching apart from Duane Litfin's monograph, *Paul's Theology of Preaching*, and the older work of Jerome Murphy-O'Connor, *Paul on Preaching*.[1] This is a remarkable lacuna, given the importance of preaching in Paul's ministry. This volume, then, seeks to address an important aspect of Paul's ministry that has significant implications for contemporary preaching. As readers will discover, this book is no mere academic work but a study addressed to contemporary preachers seeking a fuller understanding of the meaning and purpose of their ministry to proclaim God's word.

I am indebted to my former colleague at the Catholic University of America, Francis J. Moloney, and to my good friends, Ronald D. Witherup and Marsha Wilfong, who took the time to carefully

1. Duane Litfin, *Paul's Theology of Preaching: The Apostle's Challenge to the Art of Persuasion in Ancient Corinth* (Downers Grove, IL: IVP Academic, 2015); and Jerome Murphy-O'Connor, *Paul on Preaching* (New York: Sheed and Ward, 1964).

read this manuscript and offered me not only their helpful comments and corrections but their support and encouragement. Likewise, I am grateful to Bryan Dyer who accepted this project and to Eric Salo and the staff of Baker Academic who brought it to completion.

Finally, I have dedicated this volume to three close friends: David Joyce and Merle Lavoie, priests of the diocese of Springfield, who both died in the summer of 2022, and John P. Meier, my former colleague at the Catholic University of America, who died in the fall of that same year. I am forever grateful for their friendship.

Introduction

PAUL'S THEOLOGY OF PREACHING

And how are they to hear without someone to proclaim him?

—Romans 10:14

Does preaching matter? Although this may seem like a strange question, there is something archaic about contemporary preaching. Whereas in the modern world people proclaim their own message, be it true or false, those who preach the gospel proclaim a message that is not their own; they proclaim a message that has been entrusted to them. They preach a word that announces the truth that God has revealed in Jesus Christ.

Despite the authority of this message, there is a nagging sense that what is being proclaimed is irrelevant to daily life. It is not surprising, therefore, that preachers ask whether their ministry matters. Is preaching important? Does it have the power to change and transform the hearts and minds of those who hear the word?

I have been preaching for more than fifty years, and I too have wondered about this ministry I love so dearly. Does it make a difference in the way people live? Does it matter to them? Questions

1

such as these have led me to ask why I preach, what I should preach, and how I should preach.

I have spent a great deal of my life studying, teaching, and writing about the Pauline letters. As the years have gone by, my love for them has grown stronger. For no matter how often I read them, they unfailingly reveal something new to me. The hold they have on me comes, in no small measure, from the man who stands behind them. Driven by a powerful encounter with the risen Christ, whose followers he once persecuted, Paul poured out his life to proclaim Christ crucified and risen from the dead. The quintessential evangelist, pastor, and missionary, he traveled the Mediterranean world of Asia Minor and Greece to announce the good news of what God had done in Jesus Christ. If we were to ask him whether preaching matters, I suspect he would find our question misguided. "Of course, it matters," he would respond. "What could be more important than proclaiming the gospel about God's new creation that has broken into the world through the death and resurrection of Jesus Christ? What could be more important than calling people to live in, with, and for Christ in this new creation that is transforming our lives, even if we are not aware of it?"

Paul knew from personal experience that God was at work in Christ for the salvation of the world. He knew that, in Christ, God's future had broken into Paul's own life and the life of the world. Does preaching matter? If the gospel is true—and for Paul there could be no doubt about this—then preaching is of inestimable importance. For when the gospel is proclaimed, God's saving grace is revealed. When the gospel is proclaimed, we are invited into God's new creation in Christ. When the gospel is proclaimed, those who receive the word with a generous heart understand how the economy of God's salvation embraces not just humanity but the whole of creation.

The purpose of this small volume is to ask why, what, and how Paul preached in order to clarify why, what, and how we should preach. To be sure, our preaching is different from Paul's. Whereas most contemporary preachers are resident pastors who preach to their congregation in order to strengthen faith, Paul was a missionary pastor who, in addition to strengthening the congregations he established, sought to preach the gospel where it had not yet been proclaimed. He is in a unique position, therefore, to teach us *why* we preach, *what* we ought to preach, and *how* we should proclaim the gospel. To answer these three questions, I examine the Pauline letters with a view to what they say about preaching. I also draw on the witness of the Acts of the Apostles, which provides examples of Paul's preaching as relayed by Luke.[1] My primary focus, however, will be on what Paul himself says about his preaching and what his understanding of preaching means for our preaching today.

Paul's Theology of Preaching

A good way to understand Paul's theology of preaching is to reflect on a series of questions that he raises in Romans 10:14–15:

> But how are they to call on one in whom they have not believed? And how are they to believe in one of whom they have never heard? And how are they to hear without someone to proclaim him? And how are they to proclaim him unless they are sent? As it is written, "How beautiful are the feet of those who bring good news!"

This brief but extraordinary passage is part of a discussion that occurs in Romans 9–11, where Paul must deal with an issue that calls into question the gospel he preaches: if the gospel is the fulfillment of God's promises to Israel, why has Israel failed to believe that Jesus is the Christ? Has the word of God failed? Given the importance of this question, it will be helpful to review

---

1. Although Paul's sermons in Acts are literary creations of Luke, they give us insight into how he may have preached in certain circumstances, as I will show.

Paul's answer in Romans 9–11 before we turn to the text of Romans 10:14–15.[2]

The word of God has not failed. Paul begins his discussion of Israel's failure to believe by insisting that even though the majority of his compatriots have not believed in the gospel, the word of God has not failed. For just as God worked on the principle of election and mercy in Israel's past, so God is working in the same way at the present time, with the result that a remnant of Israel has believed in Jesus as the Messiah (Rom. 9:6–13). In addition to this remnant, the gentiles, who formerly did not belong to God's people, have become God's people through faith in the Jewish Messiah (9:14–29). The word of God has not failed because God is dealing with Israel in the way God has always dealt with Israel: on the basis of mercy and election. Through this process of mercy and election, God is creating a community of Jews and gentiles who confess Jesus as Lord and Messiah.

Israel failed to attain righteousness. After showing that God's word has not failed (Rom. 9:30–33), Paul asks why the gentiles, who were not striving for righteousness, have attained it, whereas Israel, who was striving for a righteousness based on the law, did not. Paul argues that Israel tripped over the stumbling stone that is Christ. Instead of pursuing the righteousness that God offers through faith in Christ, Israel sought to establish its own righteousness through the law.

Christ is the goal of the law. Paul expresses his heartfelt desire and prayer for his fellow Israelites because they are zealous for God (Rom. 10:1–4). Their zeal, however, is misguided because, ignorant of the righteousness that God offers them in Christ, they seek to establish their own righteousness on the basis of doing the law. They have not understood that the law attained its goal in Christ (10:4).

---

2. I have summarized Paul's line of argument in my commentary, *Romans*, Paideia: Commentaries on the New Testament (Grand Rapids: Baker Academic, 2010), 211–80. For an accessible summary of Paul's argument, see Ronald D. Witherup, *Scripture and Tradition in the Letters of Paul*, Biblical Studies from the Catholic Biblical Association of America (New York: Paulist Press, 2021), 46–79.

Righteousness comes from faith. Reading Israel's scriptures
in the light of Christ (Rom. 10:5–13), Paul argues that Moses
spoke prophetically of the righteousness that comes from faith
when he wrote: "Do not say in your heart, 'Who will ascend into
heaven?' (that is, to bring Christ down) or 'Who will descend into
the abyss?' (that is, to bring Christ up from the dead)" (Rom.
10:6–7, quoting Deut. 30:14).[3] There is no need to search for this
righteousness because Moses testifies that "the word is near you,
in your mouth and in your heart" (Rom. 10:8, quoting Deut.
20:12–13). The "word" of which Moses was speaking, Paul says,
is the word of faith that he (Paul) proclaims. According to Paul,
Moses spoke of the gospel and the righteousness that comes from
faith in the gospel. Consequently, those who confess with their
lips that Jesus is Lord and believe in their heart that God raised
him from the dead will be saved.

All who call on the name of the Lord will be saved. Finally,
Paul cites a text from the prophets to show that "everyone who
calls on the name of the Lord shall be saved" (Rom. 10:13, quoting Joel 2:32). But whereas Joel had in view "the Lord" who is
YHWH, Paul has in view the Lord Jesus who was given the title
"Lord" (*Kyrios*) at his exaltation (see Phil. 2:9–11). Accordingly,
he interprets the text to mean that those who call on the name of
the *Lord Jesus* will be saved.

After quoting Joel, Paul asks a series of questions that might
explain why Israel has not believed in the gospel:

> But how are they to *call*
> on one in whom they have not *believed*?
> And how are they to *believe*
> in one of whom they have never *heard*?
> And how are they to *hear*
> without someone to *proclaim* him?

3. It is evident from Paul's introductory interpretive comments that he is *rereading*
Israel's scriptures in the light of his faith in the risen Christ.

And how are they to *proclaim* him
    unless they are *sent*?
As it is written, "How beautiful are the feet of those who
    bring good news!" (Rom. 10:14–15)

With these four questions, Paul reveals how he envisions his
ministry of preaching. But instead of starting at the beginning of
the process (the sending of the preacher to proclaim the gospel),
he begins with the goal of preaching (to bring people to call on
the name of the Lord).

If we reverse the order of Paul's questions, we arrive at his
understanding of the ministry of preaching: (1) Preaching begins
when someone is *sent* to proclaim the message of the gospel.
(2) The one sent *proclaims* the message of the gospel to others,
especially to those who have not heard it. (3) Those who *hear* the
message are confronted with a decision that will profoundly alter
their lives. They must decide whether they will believe or reject the
word that has been proclaimed to them. (4) If those who hear the
gospel embrace the message in faith, they will *call* on the name
of the Lord (Jesus) and be saved. Consequently, Paul's theology
of preaching can be summarized in this way:

The preacher is *sent*.
    The message is *proclaimed*.
        What is proclaimed is *believed*.
            Those who believe *call on the name of the Lord* and
            are saved.

The Sending of the Preacher

The ministry of preaching begins when someone is entrusted
and sent with a message to proclaim: namely, the good news of
what God has done in the saving death and life-giving resurrection of Jesus Christ. The obvious but often forgotten corollary to

this statement is that those who proclaim the gospel cannot send themselves. They cannot commission themselves to be ministers of the word because they are not proclaiming their own message but a message entrusted to them by another. That message could ultimately be described as the revelation of the mystery and plan of God in Jesus Christ. Because it is revealed, those who proclaim this message have not devised it for themselves. Those who proclaim the gospel have been sent and commissioned by another with a message that has been revealed and entrusted to them. Why they have been chosen to proclaim this good news is not immediately apparent. Others could have been chosen. But for reasons that remain hidden, God chooses who will be sent to proclaim the good news. At the time of the Babylonian exile, for example, God chose the prophet Isaiah to proclaim the good news of Israel's return from exile (Isa. 40:6).[4] Centuries later, Jesus was sent by the Father with the gospel of God, the good news of the inbreaking of God's kingdom (Mark 1:14–15). During his ministry, Jesus chose disciples to announce the kingdom (6:13–15), and after his resurrection, he commissioned them to proclaim his death and resurrection to the whole world (Matt. 28:19–20). Ever since, ministers of the word have been commissioned by the church through baptism and/or ordination to proclaim a message that has been entrusted to them: the good news of Christ's death and resurrection, with all that this implies for the new creation that Jesus Christ has inaugurated by his resurrection from the dead.

Hearing the Proclamation

Preachers are *sent* to proclaim a message that has been entrusted to them so that others may hear and believe what has been

4. Although Isaiah 40 dates centuries after the death of the prophet Isaiah, the canonical text attributes the authorship of the *entire* book to him. This is why I refer to Isaiah as the one who was called to proclaim the good news that the time of exile has ended.

proclaimed. Preaching, as Paul understands it, is an encounter between those who proclaim the word and those who hear the word. Because this message is not the personal word of those who proclaim it but a word entrusted to them, the message they bring has the power to lead others to life or death, depending on whether it is received with faith or is rejected.[5] It is a message of grace and salvation that can be accepted or refused. In addition to proclaiming the gospel, therefore, hearing the gospel plays a central role in Paul's theology of preaching. For those who hear the gospel are confronted with a word of salvation that transcends the words of those who proclaim it; it is the word of the one who sent them, a word that calls for the obedience of faith. Hearing and obeying this word is a matter of life and death.

Throughout his letters, Paul recalls how the communities he formed heard and received the word of the gospel he proclaimed to them. For example, he reminds the Thessalonians how they received his preaching when they heard the gospel: "We also constantly give thanks to God for this, that when you received the word of God that you heard from us you accepted it not as a human word but as what it really is, God's word, which is also at work in you believers" (1 Thess. 2:13). When the Thessalonians heard Paul preach, they heard God's word in Paul's words. Paul makes a similar point when he asks the Galatians, "Did you receive the Spirit by doing the works of the law or by believing what you heard?" (Gal. 3:2).[6] The answer is obvious. The Galatians received the gift of the Spirit when they believed in the word of the gospel they heard, for it was no ordinary word they heard and believed but the word of God proclaimed to them in Paul's words. The word the preacher proclaims is more than

5. Paul describes this critical encounter in 2 Cor. 2:15–16, where he affirms that the gospel he proclaims leads to life or death depending on how it is received: "For we are the aroma of Christ to God among those who are being saved and among those who are perishing: to the one group a fragrance from death to death, to the other a fragrance from life to life. Who is qualified for these things?"

6. The Greek text *akoēs pisteōs* can be construed as "hearing with faith" or "hearing the message of faith." Either way, faith and hearing are intimately related.

a human word, even while it is communicated in human words. It is the word of God, and when it is proclaimed, those who hear it hear God's word in the human words of the preacher, a word that offers them an opportunity to believe.

Faith in What Is Heard

The desired outcome of hearing the word is a deep, abiding faith that the word is trustworthy because the one who sent the preacher is trustworthy. Such faith plays a central role in Paul's theology of preaching. At the beginning of his letter to the Romans, he writes of the commission he received from Christ "through whom we have received grace and apostleship to bring about the obedience of faith among all the gentiles for the sake of his name, including you who are called to belong to Jesus Christ" (Rom. 1:5–6). The obedience of faith, which leads to calling on the name of the Lord, is the desired outcome of Paul's preaching among the gentiles.[7] The gospel is "God's saving power for everyone who believes" (1:16) so that gentiles as well as Jews are justified (put in a right relationship with God) on the basis of trusting faith rather than on the basis of the law. It is not surprising, then, that Paul praises the faith of his converts. Their faith is an indication that they have heard the preached word and accepted it as the word of God rather than as a mere human word.[8]

Calling on the Name of the Lord

Faith, however, is only the penultimate step in the ministry of preaching. Those who hear and entrust themselves to the word

7. The "obedience of faith" (*hypakoēn pisteōs*, Rom. 1:5) can be construed as the obedience that faith brings about or the obedience that is faith. In both instances, faith in God and obedience to God are intimately related.

8. Note how Paul commends the faith, love, and hope of the Thessalonians: "We always give thanks to God for all of you and mention you in our prayers, constantly remembering before our God and Father your work of faith and labor of love and steadfastness of hope in our Lord Jesus Christ" (1 Thess. 1:2–3).

must call on the name of the Lord. The expression Paul employs in Romans 10:13 ("calls on the name of the Lord") comes from Joel 2:32 ("Everyone who calls on the name of the Lord shall be saved"). Peter also uses this text in his speech at Pentecost to explain the outpouring of the Holy Spirit (Acts 2:21). Like Paul, Peter understands "the Lord" to be the risen, exalted Christ. To call on the name of the Lord, therefore, is to confess that Jesus is Lord. Jesus is Lord because God exalted him and gave him the name (*Kyrios*, Lord) that is above every other name, so that at the name of Jesus "every knee should bend, in heaven and on earth and under the earth, and every tongue should confess that Jesus Christ is Lord, to the glory of God the Father" (Phil. 2:10–11). The expression "everyone who calls on the name of the Lord" describes those who believe in Jesus as Lord and Messiah. In his greeting to the Corinthians, for example, Paul writes, "To the church of God that is in Corinth, to those who are sanctified in Christ Jesus, called to be saints, together with all those who in every place *call on the name of our Lord Jesus Christ*, both their Lord and ours" (1 Cor. 1:2). A similar description is found in 2 Timothy 2:22, where Paul instructs Timothy, "Shun youthful passions and pursue righteousness, faith, love, and peace, along with those who call on the Lord from a pure heart."[9] The desired outcome of preaching is to bring those who believe the gospel to the confession of the church that Jesus Christ is Lord by virtue of his death and resurrection.

The Failure to Believe

The outcome of preaching, however, is never assured, since those who hear the word can reject it, as did many of Paul's compatriots. After posing the four questions that outline his theology of

---

9. Although 1 Timothy may have been written by someone else in Paul's name (perhaps a member of the Pauline circle), what it says here is faithful to Paul's thought.

preaching, he explains why his compatriots have not believed the gospel that has been preached to them:

> But not all have obeyed the good news, for Isaiah says, "Lord, who has believed our message?" So faith comes from what is heard, and what is heard comes through the word of Christ.
> But I ask, have they not heard? Indeed they have:
>
> > "Their voice has gone out to all the earth
> > and their words to the ends of the world."
>
> Again I ask, did Israel not understand? First Moses says,
>
> > "I will use those who are not a nation to make you jealous;
> > with a foolish nation I will provoke you."
>
> Then Isaiah is so bold as to say,
>
> > "I have been found by those who did not seek me;
> > I have shown myself to those who did not ask for me."
>
> But of Israel he says, "All day long I have held out my hands to a disobedient and contrary people." (Rom. 10:16–21)

Paul compares what is happening now with what occurred in the time of the prophet Isaiah. Although Isaiah proclaimed the word the Lord entrusted to him, his compatriots did not believe what he proclaimed, just as Paul's compatriots do not believe what he preaches.

Paul asks whether Israel has heard the message of the gospel. Employing a quotation from Psalm 19, he affirms that the voice of those sent to preach the gospel has gone to the ends of the earth.

Paul then offers another potential excuse for Israel's failure. Perhaps Israel has not understood the gospel. In response, Paul affirms that Moses foresaw that God would make Israel jealous of the gentiles, and Isaiah foresaw that the gentiles, who were not seeking God, would find God. Israel, however, has been a disobedient and contrary people.[10] Accordingly, even though the word of the gospel has been proclaimed to Israel, Israel has not believed and called on the name of the Lord, thereby reminding preachers that the outcome of their preaching is never assured.

A Theology of Preaching

Although it was not Paul's purpose to develop a theology of preaching, what he writes in Romans 10:14–15 offers insight into his understanding of what it means to preach the gospel. Deeply aware that the word is proclaimed by frail human beings, Paul grounds preaching in a commission that evangelists have received from another. Evangelists have been *sent* by God to announce a message entrusted to them, not their own message. They do this so that others will *hear* the word that has been entrusted to them, God's word in human words. When others hear that message, they are confronted with a word that has the power to bring them to salvation, a word they can embrace, ignore, or reject. Should they accept the word they hear in faith, it will empower them to *call* on the name of the Lord Jesus. And calling on him, they will be saved and united with all who call on the name of the Lord. The structure of Paul's theology of preaching is grounded in a series of interconnected movements: (1) the commissioning and sending of the preacher, (2) the proclamation of the entrusted message of the gospel, (3) the hearing of the word by those to whom it is proclaimed, (4) faith in the word that one hears, and (5) calling on the name of the Lord in whom the hearer believes.

10. In Romans 11, Paul arrives at a solution for the failure of Israel to believe. God has not rejected Israel, but a hardening has come over part of Israel as the gentiles become included as God's people. But God's promises are irrevocable, and when the Messiah comes forth from Zion at the parousia, Israel will be saved.

What can this teach us about our preaching? If we approach the word we proclaim as merely a human word, preaching doesn't matter. For while it may be of some value to us, it cannot lead those who hear it to salvation. But if Paul's understanding of what happens in the act of proclamation is true, then preaching is profoundly important. Preaching matters because it proclaims God's word, not our word. Preaching matters because those who proclaim the word have been sent to preach, not because they have decided to preach. Preaching matters because it has the power to establish an encounter between the word and the hearer of the word. When this happens, those who hear the word are able to call on the name of the Lord and be saved. Yes, preaching matters, and it can transform those who hear God's word through the human words of the preacher.

To preach effectively, we must remember that we have been entrusted with a message that is not our own; we have been entrusted with the word of life found in the very scriptures from which we proclaim. Consequently, just as Paul remained faithful to the gospel that was entrusted to him by Christ, so we must remain faithful to the scriptures entrusted to us by the church.

Preparation to proclaim the gospel requires a profound intimacy with the word of sacred scripture, an intimacy born of a lifelong study and engagement with the word in silence, in prayer, and in exegesis. It is only when we turn to the text again and again that she reveals her secrets to us.[11] The text that we quickly read once or twice will not reveal her secrets to us. The text that we think we already know will not reveal her secrets to us. The text that we think we can control will not reveal her secrets to us. The text reveals her secrets only to those who return to her again and again; for the text is a living word that already knows us better than we know her.

---

11. I have purposely referred to the text using the feminine pronoun (she, her) because I am making the point that I view her as my lover, a living text who reveals her secrets to me to the extent that I spend time with her and become intimate with her.

Paul's ministry of proclaiming Christ changed and transformed him as well as those who embraced his preaching of the word. As he proclaimed Christ in new and different circumstances, he grew in his own understanding of the gospel that was revealed to him in Christ. Something similar happens to us when we engage the word over the course of a lifetime. The time we spend preparing to preach, in prayer and exegesis, becomes a spiritual exercise that changes and transforms us so that what we proclaim is not our word but the very word of God. When this happens, preaching matters and it changes lives.

In the chapters that follow, I discuss the origin of Paul's preaching in the light of his call and conversion (chap. 1), the content of Paul's preaching in the light of the gospel he received from the risen Christ (chap. 2), how Paul sought to preach in a way that mirrored the gospel he proclaimed (chap. 3), Paul's understanding of preaching as the ministry of a new covenant (chap. 4), and seven ways in which we can preach in a Pauline manner (chap. 5).

1

Why Paul Preached

For an obligation is laid on me.

—1 Corinthians 9:16

Why did Paul preach? To answer this question, I turn to the defining moment of Paul's life, his call and conversion.[1] That moment, more than any other, defined Paul, his preaching, and the message he proclaimed. Called to be an apostle of the risen Christ, he was set apart to proclaim a message entrusted to him that he could never have imagined proclaiming before his encounter with Christ: that the crucified Jesus was God's Anointed One, the Messiah, the Son of God through whom God reconciled the world to himself. After a review of how Luke presents Paul's call in the

1. The precise language here is often disputed, with many arguing that Paul was not "converted" from one religion to another but "called" as were the prophets of Israel. While this is true, there is some value in retaining the language of conversion since Paul's prophetic call dramatically changed how he lived and understood God's activity in his life and the life of the world. Accordingly, I use both terms with the understanding that after his call Paul's life and behavior dramatically changed. On this point, see Alan F. Segal, *Paul the Convert: The Apostolate and Apostasy of Saul the Pharisee* (New Haven: Yale University Press, 1990).

Acts of the Apostles, I consider a number of texts in the Pauline letters that explain why Paul proclaimed that Jesus is the Christ. And I conclude with some reflections on what Paul's call implies for preaching today.

God's Chosen Instrument

Luke provides three accounts of Paul's call and conversion in order to highlight the importance of this event in Paul's life for his understanding of Christ and how the risen Lord altered Paul's life. Acts 9 recounts Paul's encounter with the risen Christ on his way to Damascus, his baptism by Ananias, and then his proclamation of Jesus as the Messiah. Paul later recounts these events in a speech, defending himself before an angry crowd in Jerusalem (Acts 22). And he recounts them in another speech in Caesarea before the Jewish king Agrippa and the Roman governor Festus (Acts 26). In what follows, I show how Paul's encounter with the risen Lord lies at the origin of his preaching.[2]

Luke's first account of Paul's encounter with Jesus occurs shortly after the stoning of Stephen, to which Paul consented (Acts 8:1) and after which he was working to destroy the church by handing over for punishment those who believed Jesus to be the Messiah (8:3).[3] When we next meet Paul, he is on his way to Damascus to bring back to Jerusalem those Jews who were following this new way. Luke's description of what happened is brief but vivid:

Now as he was going along and approaching Damascus, suddenly a light from heaven flashed around him. He fell to the ground and

2. The historicity of the Lukan accounts of Paul's call/conversion and the relationship of these three accounts to each other are complicated issues that I do not discuss in this chapter. I proceed on the assumption that even though these narratives are Lukan compositions rather than eyewitness accounts, they provide us with a profound theological understanding of why Paul preached the gospel.

3. Although Luke uses Paul's Jewish name "Saul" in this part of the narrative, I use Paul for the sake of clarity.

heard a voice saying to him, "Saul, Saul, why do you persecute me?"
He asked, "Who are you, Lord?" The reply came, "I am Jesus,
whom you are persecuting. But get up and enter the city, and you
will be told what you are to do." The men who were traveling with
him stood speechless because they heard the voice but saw no one.
Saul got up from the ground, and though his eyes were open, he
could see nothing; so they led him by the hand and brought him
into Damascus. For three days he was without sight and neither
ate nor drank. (Acts 9:3–9)

Paul encounters the risen Jesus in an experience of flashing
light from heaven, but he does not know who is speaking until
Jesus identifies himself as the one whom Paul is persecuting by
pursuing his followers.

The scene shifts from Paul to Ananias, a devout believer living
in Damascus, who receives a vision from the Lord to go to a man
of Tarsus named Saul. Although Ananias protests because of what
Paul has done to the believers in Jerusalem and what he proposes
to do in Damascus, the Lord insists: "Go, for he is an instrument
whom I have chosen to bring my name before gentiles and kings
and before the people of Israel; I myself will show him how much
he must suffer for the sake of my name" (9:15–16). And so Ananias
goes to Paul and explains that he has been sent by the Lord Jesus,
who appeared to him so that Paul might regain his sight and be
filled with the Holy Spirit.

After being baptized by Ananias, Paul proclaims in the syna-
gogues in Damascus, to the dismay of all, that Jesus is the Son
of God. He becomes stronger and confounds the Jews there by
proving that Jesus was truly the Messiah (9:20–22). When Paul's
life is threatened in Damascus, he returns to Jerusalem, where
even those who believe in Jesus do not accept that he has become
a believer. Barnabas intervenes, however, and brings Paul to the
apostles and describes how he spoke boldly in the name of Jesus
in Damascus. As the scene ends, we find Paul arguing with the
Hellenists that Jesus is the Messiah (9:26–30).

This account reveals the intimate relationship between Paul's call and his preaching. Paul preaches that Jesus is the Son of God, the Messiah, because the crucified one appeared to him. The dissonance between who Paul was and who he has become could not be greater. There is no way to explain the power with which he proclaims Jesus apart from his encounter with the risen Lord. Paul did not proclaim his own message but a message entrusted to him. He did not decide to preach; he was sent to preach.

In Acts 22 Luke tells the story of Paul's call from Paul's own point of view, Paul having been taken into custody by the Romans for inciting a riot in Jerusalem.[4] Paul persuades the Roman tribune to let him address the Jewish crowd. Speaking in Hebrew, he defends himself by reminding his compatriots of his impeccable Jewish background. Educated at the feet of the eminent Gamaliel in the Mosaic law, he was as zealous for God's law as they were. Indeed, he was more zealous, since he persecuted "the followers of this Way" (22:4) by arresting and bringing believers to Jerusalem for punishment. But as Paul was on his way to Damascus, the risen Christ appeared to him, asking why he was persecuting him. Commanded by the risen one, he went to Damascus, where Ananias explained the significance of this encounter:

> Brother Saul, regain your sight! . . . The God of our ancestors has chosen you to know his will, to see the Righteous One, and to hear his own voice, for you will be his witness to all the world of what you have seen and heard. And now why do you delay? Get up, be baptized, and have your sins washed away, calling on his name. (Acts 22:13–16)

4. In Acts 22 and 26, we are hearing Paul's account of the events. That the two chapters differ in some details from what Luke writes in Acts 9, and that they differ from each other, is because Paul is narrating his account to different audiences for different purposes. My primary purpose is to ascertain *why* Paul began to preach the gospel, the followers of which he once persecuted.

Paul then relates a second encounter he had with the risen Christ in the temple of Jerusalem, not mentioned in Acts 9, in which the Lord commissions him:

> After I had returned to Jerusalem and while I was praying in the temple, I fell into a trance and saw Jesus saying to me, "Hurry and get out of Jerusalem quickly, because they will not accept your testimony about me." And I said, "Lord, they themselves know that in every synagogue I imprisoned and beat those who believed in you. And while the blood of your witness Stephen was shed, I myself was standing by, approving and keeping the coats of those who killed him." Then he said to me, "Go, for I will send you far away to the gentiles." (Acts 22:17–21)

What is significant in this account is that Paul receives his commission to preach directly from the risen Christ, who sends him to testify before the gentiles, since his own compatriots will not accept his witness.

In Acts 26 Luke narrates a second account of Paul's call from Paul's point of view. Like the account of Acts 22, it is a defense speech. The setting here is in Caesarea before the Jewish king Agrippa and the Roman governor Festus. As in his first defense speech, Paul recounts how zealous he was for the law. He lived as a Pharisee, the strictest sect of his people, and as a Pharisee, he hoped for the resurrection of the dead. Now that the risen Lord had revealed himself to him, Paul knows that the resurrection of the dead has begun in the resurrection of Jesus the Messiah, and so he cries out,

> And now I stand here on trial on account of my hope in the promise made by God to our ancestors, a promise that our twelve tribes hope to attain, as they earnestly worship day and night. It is for this hope, Your Excellency, that I am accused by Jews! Why is it thought incredible by any of you that God raises the dead? (Acts 26:6–8)

Paul then describes his encounter with the risen Lord, how he saw "a light from heaven, brighter than the sun, shining around me and my companions" (26:13). This time, however, he reveals something else that Jesus said to him: "Saul, Saul, why are you persecuting me? It hurts you to kick against the goads" (26:14), a proverbial expression by which Jesus questions why Paul is resisting his destiny. The risen Lord then commissions Paul:

> I am Jesus whom you are persecuting. But get up and stand on your feet, for I have appeared to you for this purpose, to appoint you to serve and testify to the things in which you have seen me and to those in which I will appear to you. I will rescue you from your people and from the gentiles—*to whom I am sending* you to open their eyes so that they may turn from darkness to light and from the power of Satan to God, so that they may receive forgiveness of sins and a place among those who are sanctified by faith in me. (Acts 26:15–18)

The remarkable aspect of this account is its emphasis on the resurrection. The appearance of the risen Christ showed Paul the Pharisee that the resurrection of the dead has begun in Jesus the Messiah. The content of his preaching, which he received from the risen Lord, therefore, is the resurrection of the dead. His preaching deals with the promise made to Israel and for which Israel has been waiting and hoping—namely, the resurrection of the dead, which had begun in Jesus.[5]

A Revelation of Jesus Christ

Paul's most explicit description of his call in his own writings occurs in his letter to the Galatians, in which he defends his apostleship

---

5. The promise of the resurrection of the dead was derived from Paul's hope, as a Pharisee, that there would be a general resurrection of the dead. What is new is that in the light of his call, Paul believes that the general resurrection has begun in Jesus the Messiah.

and the gospel he preaches among the gentiles, as is evident from the opening words of the letter that also highlight the resurrection: "Paul an apostle—sent neither by human commission nor from human authorities but through Jesus Christ and God the Father, who raised him from the dead" (1:1). He has to defend his apostleship because rival missionaries have come to Galatia and questioned his right to be called an apostle and criticized the gospel he preaches, which does not require gentiles to be circumcised or to observe the Mosaic law. To counter their opposition, Paul recounts how he was called to be an apostle and commissioned to preach the gospel.

Paul begins his defense by insisting that his gospel is "not of human origin, for I did not receive it from a human source, nor was I taught it, but I received it through a revelation of Jesus Christ" (Gal. 1:11–12).[6] To emphasize the divine origin of his gospel and apostleship, he reminds the Galatians of his life in Judaism, when he persecuted the church and advanced in Judaism beyond his contemporaries, being far more zealous for the traditions of his ancestors than they were (Gal. 1:13–14).

> But when the one who had set me apart before I was born and called me through his grace was pleased to reveal his Son to me [*en emoi*],[7] so that I might proclaim him among the gentiles, I did not confer with any human, nor did I go up to Jerusalem to those who were already apostles before me, but I went away at once into Arabia, and afterward I returned to Damascus. (Gal. 1:15–17)

Paul makes several points in this complex sentence. First, God set Paul apart for apostleship while he was still in his mother's

6. The Greek text (*apokalypseōs Iēsou Christou*) can be construed in two ways: a revelation *about* Jesus Christ or a revelation *from* Jesus Christ. Since Paul describes God as the one who calls him (Gal. 1:15), the first may be the more precise rendering, but the second need not be excluded. The content of the revelation is Jesus Christ, and the fact that God reveals his Son to Paul indicates that it also comes from Jesus Christ.
7. The Greek (*en emoi*) can be construed as meaning "to me" or "in me." Paul does not describe his call in the dramatic way that Luke does in Acts.

womb.[8] Second, through a gracious act of divine favor, God revealed that the crucified Jesus is his Son. Third, the purpose of this revelation was that Paul might proclaim the gospel to the gentiles. Fourth, the meaning of the revelation was so evident to Paul that it was not necessary to confer with others about its meaning. Fifth, after this revelation, Paul went to Arabia and then to Damascus, presumably to preach the gospel that had been entrusted to him.[9]

Although Paul's description of his call here is brief compared to the accounts in Acts, it provides the Galatians with the assurance they need about the legitimacy of his apostleship and the trustworthiness of his preaching. Paul would never have chosen to preach a gospel that proclaimed a crucified Messiah and did not require circumcision nor doing the works of the law. Only a call from God the Father and Jesus Christ can explain why he proclaims this gospel to gentiles. Rather than preach his own message, Paul proclaims a gospel that was entrusted to him at his call.[10]

An Obligation to Preach the Gospel

The realization that he had been called to preach the crucified Jesus impressed on Paul a sense of mission and obligation. At the beginning of Romans, for example, he writes,

> Paul, a servant of Christ Jesus, called to be an apostle, set apart for the gospel of God, which he promised beforehand through his prophets in the holy scriptures, the gospel concerning his Son,

8. Here there are echoes of the calls of the servant (Isa. 49:1) and of Jeremiah (Jer. 1:5).

9. What Paul did in Arabia is debated. Did he go there to reflect on what had happened to him, or did he begin his preaching of the gospel there? I suggest that this was the beginning of Paul's preaching of the gospel.

10. This does not mean that Paul received every detail of the gospel he would later proclaim at the moment of his call. He certainly grew in his understanding of the gospel. But in the divine revelation of Jesus as the Son of God, he received the essence of the gospel he would preach; namely, that the risen Lord is the crucified Jesus by whose death humanity has been justified and reconciled to God.

who was descended from David according to the flesh and was declared to be Son of God with power according to the spirit of holiness by resurrection from the dead, Jesus Christ our Lord, through whom we have received grace and apostleship to bring about the obedience of faith among all the gentiles for the sake of his name, including you who are called to belong to Jesus Christ. (Rom. 1:1–6)

In this letter opening, Paul introduces himself, as he did in Galatians 1:15, as someone who has been "set apart" to bring gentiles to the obedience of faith in Jesus Christ. Because he has been selected for this work, he understands his ministry in this way: "I am obligated both to Greeks and to barbarians, both to the wise and to the foolish, hence my eagerness to proclaim the gospel to you also who are in Rome" (Rom. 1:14–15). This sense of obligation, we can assume, derives from his call.

In his letter to the Corinthians, Paul emphasizes the centrality of preaching in his ministry, reminding the Corinthians, who were aligning themselves with the one who baptized them, that "Christ did not send me to baptize but to proclaim the gospel—and not with eloquent wisdom, so that the cross of Christ might not be emptied of its power" (1 Cor. 1:17). This statement is intended not to denigrate the importance of baptism but to remind the Corinthians of what is central to Paul's ministry: the preaching of the gospel that leads to faith and baptism.[11] Thus, while Paul did baptize others, his experience of being called by Christ led him to define the purpose of his ministry in terms of preaching the gospel rather than baptizing.

Paul reveals his sense of obligation to preach the gospel in 1 Corinthians 9, where he presents himself as an example of someone who has set aside his legitimate rights as an apostle in order to win as many people as possible for the gospel. Among the rights

11. Paul affirms the importance of baptism for the Christian life in his discussion of baptism in Romans 6.

he could have insisted on, but did not, was the right to be supported by the Corinthian community (see 1 Cor. 9:12–14). He then explains why he has not insisted on these rights:

> But I have made no use of any of these rights, nor am I writing this so that they may be applied in my case. Indeed, I would rather die than that—no one will deprive me of my ground for boasting! If I proclaim the gospel, this gives me no ground for boasting, for an obligation is laid on me [*anagkē gar moi epikeitai*], and woe to me if I do not proclaim the gospel! For if I do this of my own will, I have a wage, but if not of my own will, I am entrusted with a commission. What then is my wage? Just this: that in my proclamation I may make the gospel free of charge, so as not to make full use of my rights in the gospel. (1 Cor. 9:15–18)

Paul has not insisted on his rights as an apostle because of his obligation to proclaim the gospel imposed on him when he was called. The decision to preach the gospel was not his. This obligation will always remain even if Paul refuses to accept it, and so he can approach it willingly or unwillingly. If he accepts it begrudgingly, he will carry out his ministry as something imposed on him against his will. But if he embraces it willingly by not asking for recompense, his reward will be that he preaches without requiring support from the Corinthian community. To show his freedom while under obligation, therefore, Paul does not insist on his apostolic rights. He seeks to make himself accessible to as many people as he can by not insisting on his rights as an apostle so that he can save as many as possible. He writes, "I do it all for the sake of the gospel, so that I might become a partner in it" (1 Cor. 9:23).

Paul's sense of obligation to preach derives from the unique circumstance of his call. He knew that prior to preaching the gospel he had persecuted the church of God. The call he received, then, was an extraordinary gift of unmerited grace that imposed an obligation on him, which he accepted by preaching the gospel free of charge.

Appointed and Entrusted with the Gospel

Paul's sense of obligation to preach is also on display in 1 Timothy, where he again refers to his call.[12] But whereas in Galatians Paul emphasizes his zealousness for the law in order to highlight the change brought about in him through his call, in 1 Timothy he recalls the violence that resulted from his persecution of the gospel in order to highlight the extraordinary mercy God bestowed on him in calling him to preach the gospel.

> I am grateful to Christ Jesus our Lord, who has strengthened me, because he considered me faithful and appointed me to his service, even though I was formerly a blasphemer, a persecutor, and a man of violence. But I received mercy because I had acted ignorantly in unbelief, and the grace of our Lord overflowed for me with the faith and love that are in Christ Jesus. The saying is sure and worthy of full acceptance: that Christ Jesus came into the world to save sinners—of whom I am the foremost. But for that very reason I received mercy, so that in me, as the foremost, Jesus Christ might display the utmost patience as an example to those who would come to believe in him for eternal life. (1 Tim. 1:12–16)

Paul's commission to preach is an obligation born of grace and mercy for the purpose of making him an example of God's great mercy to sinners. For if God could make the blasphemer and persecutor of the gospel an evangelist, there is hope for all sinners.

In 2 Timothy Paul reminds his young coworker how he (Paul) was appointed a herald, an apostle, and a teacher: "For this gospel I was appointed a herald and an apostle and a teacher, and for this reason I suffer as I do. But I am not ashamed, for I know the one in whom I have put my trust, and I am sure that he is able

---

12. Paul may not be the author of 1 Timothy, and this letter may have been written by another in his name. My concern, however, is what the Pauline letters say about Paul's preaching. Even if some letters were not written by Paul, they still provide us with an insight into the content of his preaching.

to guard the deposit I have entrusted to him" (2 Tim. 1:11–12). The word "herald" (*kēpyx*), which in the Pauline writings occurs only here and in 1 Timothy 2:7, refers to someone who makes an official proclamation, whether civil or religious.[13] Heralds do not proclaim their own message. They proclaim what has been entrusted to them just as it was given to them. They are not to change or embellish what they have received but to proclaim it faithfully, in a loud and clear voice, for all to hear. By designating himself as a herald of the gospel, Paul shows that he is under an obligation to preach the message that God entrusted to him through an act of mercy and grace.

Called to Preach the Hidden Mystery

In the letter to the Ephesians, Paul provides us with a profound understanding of his ministry. He presupposes that his audience has heard of the commission of God's grace (3:2) given to him for their sake. This commission is the stewardship entrusted to him when God revealed the mystery (3:3) of Christ to him.[14] This mystery, hidden from previous generations, is that the gentiles have become members of the body of Christ (the church) and sharers in the promise through the gospel Paul preaches. Although Paul presents himself as the least of God's people, "the saints" (3:8), he has become a "servant" (3:7) of this gospel because of the gift of grace given to him. His task is to make known, through his preaching, the plan of God, which is the mystery of Christ, hidden for ages, so that the wisdom of God revealed in Christ might be made known to all. I have italicized words and phrases in the text below that highlight Paul's sense of being called.

13. It is interesting that in this text "herald" occurs before "apostle," whereas in 1 Cor. 12:28 "apostle" occurs first in the list of church ministries.
14. In 1 Cor. 4:1 Paul refers to himself and other apostles as "servants of Christ and stewards of God's mysteries."

This is the reason that I, Paul, am a prisoner for Christ Jesus for the sake of you gentiles, for surely you have already heard of *the commission of God's grace that was given me* for you and how *the mystery was made known to me by revelation*, as I wrote above in a few words, a reading of which will enable you to perceive *my understanding of the mystery of Christ*. In former generations *this mystery* was not made known to humankind, as it has now been revealed to his holy apostles and prophets by the Spirit: that is, the gentiles have become fellow heirs, members of the same body, and sharers in the promise in Christ Jesus through the gospel.

Of this gospel I have become a servant according to the gift of God's grace that was given me by the working of his power. Although I am the very least of all the saints, *this grace was given to me to bring to the gentiles the news of the boundless riches of Christ* and to make everyone see *what is the plan of the mystery hidden for ages in God*, who created all things, so that through the church the wisdom of God in its rich variety might now be made known to the rulers and authorities in the heavenly places. This was in accordance with the eternal purpose that he has carried out in Christ Jesus our Lord, in whom we have access in boldness and confidence through faith in him. I pray, therefore, that you may not lose heart over my sufferings for you; they are your glory. (Eph. 3:1–13)

Ephesians provides another way to understand why Paul preaches the gospel. His call came the moment that the mystery of Christ, hidden for ages, was revealed to him. At his call, he became a minister and steward of the gospel, commissioned to make known to others the divine economy of salvation revealed in Christ. By preaching the gospel Paul reveals a mystery hidden for ages, revealed to him and other apostles, that shows the gentiles their role in the divine economy. By using the language of "mystery" and the concept of the divine economy of salvation, Paul shows that he is not preaching his own message but the mystery hidden and revealed in Christ for the sake of the gentiles as well as the Jews.

Why We Preach

We who preach must ask *why* we preach. What is our motivation for proclaiming the gospel? What inspires us to preach week after week? There are, to be sure, many answers. But the fundamental answer has to do with a sense of receiving a call and commission to preach. We preach not because we decided to do so. We preach because we have been sent and commissioned by another. Understood in this way, there is a burden to our preaching, and it is not something we can easily set aside without being unfaithful to our calling. It is not something we can decide to do from time to time. It is a mission, a commission, a stewardship, a ministry graciously given for the sake of the gospel and the church. In my own tradition (Roman Catholicism), this commission to preach comes with ordination, or in the case of lay preachers of the gospel, with a specific commission from the church.[15] Why we have been given this commission is a mystery. Others might preach more eloquently and more effectively than us. But we who have been called know that, despite our inadequacy, we have been entrusted with a stewardship.

Understanding why we preach is important, lest we preach for the wrong reasons. If we do not have a deep sense of mission and call, if preaching is something we do occasionally or when we feel the need to, something is amiss. Paul knows that he has been sent to preach. He understands that an obligation has been imposed on him. And as a result, he knows that he is the herald of a gospel that has been entrusted to him to proclaim the mystery of God's plan of salvation. When we come to a similar understanding of our ministry, our reason for preaching and the content of our preaching are changed and transformed by the pattern of the teaching that has been handed on to us by those who have gone before us.

15. I am aware all Christians are called to proclaim the gospel to the world by virtue of their baptism, but here I am primarily concerned with those who preach in a ministerial capacity as ordained clergy.

An example is found in 2 Timothy 4:1–8, a text in which Paul gives a solemn charge to his young assistant Timothy to preach the gospel. Aware that the time of his death is at hand (2 Tim. 4:6), Paul charges Timothy to "proclaim the message; be persistent whether the time is favorable or unfavorable" (v. 2), since a time is coming when people will no longer tolerate sound doctrine and will turn away from listening to the truth (vv. 3–4). Because of this, it is essential that Timothy endure his share of the suffering that comes with the gospel and fulfill his ministry by doing the work of an evangelist, preaching the gospel that Paul entrusted to him.

What Paul writes in this brief exhortation helps us understand why we preach. Like Timothy, we are the recipients of a message, the gospel, that has been handed on to us by faithful witnesses who proclaimed it before us. And just as the burden of their preaching was to proclaim what had been handed on to them, so the burden of our preaching is to proclaim the faith that the church has handed on from generation to generation so that the gospel will be heard anew.

Pauline preaching is not simply a rote recitation of the teaching we have received. Such preaching knows how to address the message of the gospel to new times and circumstances while always remaining faithful to the gospel. Rather than reducing the message to frozen formulas, such preaching shows how the gospel illumines new situations that every generation faces. We who proclaim the word today are spiritual descendants of Timothy to the extent that we seek to fulfill our ordination and baptismal commission to preach the gospel. Like Timothy, we have been instructed to remain faithful to the word, whether it is convenient or not, until the Lord's appearance.

Why do we preach? We preach because we have been entrusted with the gospel by those who have gone before us, as was Timothy and so many other witnesses after him. We preach because we have been commissioned to do so by our baptism and/or ordination. We preach not because *we* have decided to do so but because we have received a call and commission to do so.

2

What Paul Preached

But we proclaim Christ crucified.

—1 Corinthians 1:23

In the previous chapter, I explored how Paul's preaching was rooted in his call to be an apostle of Jesus Christ.[1] In this chapter, I take up a question that is closely related to the question of *why* Paul preached; namely, *what* did he preach, and what was the content of his proclamation? These questions are intertwined because the one who commissioned Paul to be his apostle defined the content of his preaching.

Paul summarizes the content of his preaching with the word "gospel," which he employs in a variety of ways—for example, "the gospel of God," "the gospel of Christ," "my gospel."[2] These

1. An apostle is, as the word itself means, one who has been "sent" on a mission.
2. In some instances he relates the gospel to God: "the gospel of God" (Rom. 1:1; 15:16; 1 Thess. 2:2, 8, 9), "the glorious gospel of the blessed God" (1 Tim. 1:11). In others, he relates the gospel to Christ: "the gospel of his Son" (Rom. 1:9), "the gospel of Christ" (Rom. 15:19; 1 Cor. 9:12; 2 Cor. 2:12; 9:13; 1 Thess. 3:2), "the gospel of the glory of Christ" (2 Cor. 4:4), "the gospel of our Lord Jesus" (2 Thess. 1:8). In still others, he relates the gospel to himself: "my gospel" (Rom. 2:16; 16:25; 2 Tim. 2:8),

phrases, though they differ, point to a common reality. The gospel is God's own good news of what God accomplished in Jesus Christ. Thus, Paul says of his preaching, "We proclaim Christ crucified" (1 Cor. 1:23), and he insists that if Christ has not been raised from the dead, then the faith of those who believe in him is futile, and they are still in their sins (1 Cor. 15:17). The gospel is the story of how God justified, reconciled, and saved the whole of humanity, gentile as well as Jew, indeed the whole of creation, by raising the crucified Jesus from the dead (Rom. 8:18–25; 1 Cor. 15:20–28).

While we can say with assurance that the content of Paul's preaching was the gospel about Christ, we do not have any examples of his preaching apart from the sermons that Luke includes in the Acts of the Apostles. What we do have are Paul's letters, which he wrote to those who believed in the initial proclamation of the gospel they heard from him or from others. Thus, it is important to distinguish between Paul's preaching and his letters, in which he provides us with further reflection on the meaning of the gospel he proclaims.[3]

In this chapter, I investigate the content of Paul's preaching from two vantage points. First, I consider two missionary sermons that Paul delivers as detailed by Luke in the Acts of the Apostles. These sermons are literary creations of Luke rather than transcriptions of Paul's preaching. Nevertheless, they give us insight

---

"our gospel" (2 Cor. 4:3), by which he does not mean his personal version of the gospel but the gospel he preaches about Christ. In other expressions, he mentions those to whom the gospel is directed or the gift that the gospel brings: "the gospel for the circumcised" and "the gospel for the uncircumcised" (Gal. 2:7), "the gospel of your salvation" (Eph. 1:13), and "the gospel of peace" (Eph. 6:15).

3. This point is made by Michael Wolter: "With the noun εὐαγγέλιον ('good tidings') and the verb εὐαγγελίσασθαί ('to proclaim good tidings'), Paul always denotes nothing other than his missionary preaching, through which he intends to gain people for Christian faith. He never employs these words with reference to the content and intention of his letters. The theological declarations and contexts of reasoning in them serve rather the *discussion* of the gospel and not its *proclamation*." Wolter, *Paul: An Outline of His Theology*, trans. Robert L. Brawley (Waco: Baylor University Press, 2015), 51 (emphasis original).

into how Luke conceived of Paul's preaching. Even though Luke is the author of these sermons, he writes with a certain authority about how the great apostle would have preached before Jews and gentiles, since he was Paul's traveling companion during part of Paul's ministry.[4] After examining these sermons, I discuss a number of texts from Paul's letters in which he reflects on the meaning and implications of the gospel he proclaims. In doing so, I hope to uncover the central themes of his preaching. I then conclude with some reflections on what Paul's preaching can teach us about our preaching today.[5]

Two Missionary Sermons

Most contemporary preaching is addressed to those who already believe. But this was not the case for Paul and other early evangelists. Paul was a missionary evangelist who preached the gospel where it had not yet been proclaimed (Rom. 15:20).

In the Acts of the Apostles, Luke provides us with many examples of missionary preaching from both Peter and Paul.[6] Even though the sermons he includes are his literary creations, they

4. While many scholars differ on this point, I am persuaded that the "we" passages in the Acts of the Apostles, which represent a shift from the third person to the first-person plural (Acts 16:10–17; 20:5–15; 21:1–18; 27:1–28:16), indicate that Luke accompanied Paul on some of his missionary journeys. On this point, see Joseph A. Fitzmyer, *The Acts of the Apostles: A New Translation with Introduction and Commentary*, Anchor Bible 31 (New York: Doubleday, 1998), 98–103.

5. For a reliable study of the speeches and sermons in Acts, see Marion L. Soards, *The Speeches in Acts: Their Content, Context, and Concerns* (Louisville: Westminster John Knox, 1994); and Christopher R. J. Holmes, *Hearing and Doing: The Speeches in Acts and the Essence of Christianity* (Waco: Baylor University Press, 2022). For an authoritative summary of the content of Paul's proclamation, see Peter Stuhlmacher, *Biblical Theology of the New Testament* (Grand Rapids: Eerdmans, 2018), 251–429.

6. Prominent among these missionary speeches are Peter's sermon at Pentecost (Acts 2:14–36), his sermon in the temple of Jerusalem (3:12–26), and his sermon to the household of Cornelius (15:34–43). While the similarity between Peter's speech at Pentecost and Paul's speech at Antioch points to Luke as their creator, it also suggests that there were similarities in the earliest Christian kerygma because of its focus on the death and resurrection of Jesus.

provide us with an understanding of how early Christian evangelists proclaimed the gospel to Jews and gentiles. From the many
sermons that Luke attributes to Paul, I have chosen two missionary sermons: his sermon in the synagogue in Antioch of Pisidia,
in which he addresses an audience of Jews and God-fearers, and
his sermon in Athens, in which he addresses gentiles. Both are
examples of missionary sermons in which the apostle proclaims
the gospel to Jews and gentiles who have not yet come to faith in
Jesus as the Christ.[7]

Paul's Preaching in Antioch of Pisidia (Acts 13:16–41)

The setting for this missionary sermon is in the synagogue in
Antioch of Pisidia, where Paul and his companions go on the
sabbath in order to worship. After the reading of the law and the
prophets, the synagogue official asks Paul and his companions if
they have a "word of exhortation" (13:15) they would like to speak
to the congregation. Paul rises and addresses the congregation of
Jews and God-fearers.[8]

Paul begins with a rehearsal of Israel's history (13:17–23) that
includes the people's deliverance from Egypt, their wandering in
the wilderness, their entry and possession of the land, and the
period of the judges that culminates in the kingship of David,
of whom God testified, "I have found David, son of Jesse, to be
a man after my heart, who will carry out all my wishes" (v. 22,
alluding to Ps. 89:20). Paul then proceeds to proclaim the gospel
by announcing that God raised up a savior for Israel, Jesus, from
the descendants of David, just as God promised.

7. For Paul's missionary sermon at Antioch, see Wenxi Zhang, *Paul among Jews:
A Study of the Meaning and Significance of Paul's Inaugural Sermon in the Syna-
gogue of Antioch in Pisidia (Acts 13:16–41) for His Missionary Work among the
Jews* (Eugene, OR: Wipf & Stock, 2011).

8. The term "God-fearers" refers to gentiles who attached themselves to the synagogue because they admired the ethical ideals of Judaism. Although they were not
circumcised or fully converted to Judaism, they were sympathetic to Judaism and
knowledgeable about many of its teachings.

After affirming that Jesus was the goal and climax of Israel's history, Paul turns to the preaching of John the Baptist (13:24–25). He explains that John testified that he was not the one whom the people supposed him to be (the Messiah). Rather, John pointed to the one who would come after him—namely, Jesus.

Having reviewed the events of Israel's history that led up to Jesus, Paul appeals to the congregation as "fellow children of Abraham and you God-fearing Gentiles," launching into an account of Jesus's passion, death, and resurrection that points to the failure of the inhabitants of Jerusalem (13:26–31). He notes that the Jerusalemites and their leaders failed to recognize Jesus as the Messiah, and by condemning him to death, they fulfilled the words of the prophets they read sabbath by sabbath, as is now happening in the synagogue in Antioch. The Jerusalemites asked Pilate to put Jesus to death, but in an act that brought about a great reversal of fortunes, God raised Jesus from the dead, and he appeared to those who now witness to his resurrection.

Having proclaimed that the events of Jesus's life and death were the culmination of Israel's history, Paul employs Psalms 2 and 16 to show the congregation that the promises God made to their ancestors have been fulfilled in the resurrection of Jesus from the dead (Acts 13:32–39).[9]

Paul concludes his sermon by assuring the congregation that the forgiveness of sins is being proclaimed to them through Jesus, by whom they are justified, a justification that was not possible under the law of Moses.[10] Finally, drawing on a quotation from

9. Paul interprets the words "You are my son; today I have begotten you" (Ps. 2:7) and "For you do not . . . let your faithful one see the Pit" (Ps. 16:10) as prophecies of Jesus's resurrection. Jesus was manifested as God's Son on the day of his resurrection when God preserved his flesh from the corruption of death.

10. Paul's statement here, "Everyone who believes is set free from all those sins from which you could not be freed [*dikaiōthēnai*, "justified"] by the law of Moses" (13:39), alludes to one of the most distinctive aspects of his theology: justification by faith. Although it is unlikely that Paul dealt with the question of justification by faith in his initial proclamation of the gospel, its presence here gives this sermon a Pauline flavor.

the prophet Habakkuk, he warns the congregation not to scoff at
what he has proclaimed to them (13:40–41).

In this missionary sermon, Paul grounds his preaching about
Jesus in Israel's history. His purpose is to show that the good
news about Jesus is the culmination of the promises God made to
Israel. The death of Jesus was not an accident of history; it was
the outworking of God's plan of salvation that offers forgiveness
of sins to those who believe the gospel. While this sermon is not
a transcription of what Paul said in the synagogue in Antioch, it
shows how he likely preached in such a setting. First, he draws a
relationship between himself and the congregation by identifying himself as a fellow Israelite. Second, he recounts the story of
Israel in a way that shows how Jesus is the promised descendant
of David, the climax of Israel's history. Next, he introduces the
kerygma, the church's proclamation of Jesus's death and resurrection for the forgiveness of sins. Finally, he calls the congregation
to repent.

Paul's Preaching in Athens (Acts 17:16–32)

Luke presents Paul's preaching at Athens in two scenes. In the
first (Acts 17:16–21), he describes how Paul debated in the synagogue with Jews and God-fearers about Jesus while at Athens.
Curious about Paul's teaching of Jesus and the "resurrection"
(which the Athenians take to be the name of a female deity), some
philosophers debate with him and lead him to the Areopagus,
where he addresses them.

In the second scene (Acts 17:22–31), Paul delivers his missionary
sermon at the Areopagus.[11] Paul begins his sermon by acknowledging the religious devotion of his audience. They worship many
gods, and they even have reserved a shrine to an unknown god.

---

11. The Areopagus could refer to the hill of the Acropolis in Athens (the hill
of Ares, the god of war, thus, Mars Hill) or it could mean that Paul was led to the
council of the Areopagus, which is the more likely meaning, according to Fitzmyer,
Acts of the Apostles, 605–6.

Turning to this shrine, Paul says that he proclaims the God whom they do not know, the God who made the world and all that is in it, the Lord of heaven and earth who does not dwell in human sanctuaries. The God whom Paul proclaims is the God of Israel, although Paul does not say this. It is the God of Israel who so ordered creation that all might seek and find God.

After establishing a relationship with his audience by praising them for their religious devotion, Paul calls them to conversion. For although God overlooked humanity's ignorance in the past, the time to repent has arrived; God has established a day when he will judge the world through a man whom he raised from the dead and appointed as judge. Paul's talk about resurrection, however, results in the audience scoffing at and dismissing him.

This missionary sermon is different from the sermon in Antioch, as is its exposition of the kerygma. Rather than grounding his sermon in Israel's history, which would have meant little to the Athenians, he grounds it in creation and in humanity's longing to know God. The content of Paul's missionary sermon in the Areopagus is that God has been revealed in the resurrection of the man God has appointed as judge. While this is not a detailed exposition of the gospel, it opens the way for those who repent to turn to the God of Israel.

The Gospel Paul Proclaims

The purpose of Paul's letter writing was different from the purpose of his initial preaching. Whereas his missionary sermons evangelized those who had not yet heard and believed in Christ, his letters were written to strengthen the faith of those who had repented and believed in the gospel. These letters, however, are closely related to Paul's proclamation of the gospel inasmuch as they expand on and develop what he preached. In this section, I investigate a number of passages in which Paul refers to his preaching so that we can get a better sense of the content of the gospel he proclaimed.

A Call to Repent and Worship the Living and True God
(1 Thessalonians)

At the outset of 1 Thessalonians, Paul speaks of the positive reception his preaching received when he proclaimed the gospel to the congregation in Thessalonica. Grateful that his proclamation found such a positive response, he says, "Our message of the gospel came to you not in word only but also in power and in the Holy Spirit and with full conviction." Thus, the Thessalonians "received the word with joy from the Holy Spirit" (1 Thess. 1:5–6). They were so receptive to Paul's preaching that their faith in the gospel became a model for others to imitate. Believers in Macedonia and Achaia were now telling Paul about the faith of the Thessalonians. He writes, "For they report about us what kind of welcome we had among you and how you turned to God from idols to serve a living and true God and to wait for his Son from heaven, whom he raised from the dead—Jesus, who rescues us from the coming wrath" (1:9–10). This brief comment gives us an insight into Paul's missionary preaching in Thessalonica, which is remarkably similar to his preaching in Athens. On the basis of what he says here, we might imagine the outline of Paul's preaching to the Thessalonians in this way:

The gods you serve are idols with no power to save you (v. 9).

The living and true God has raised his Son, Jesus, from the dead (v. 10a).

Jesus will come soon from heaven to rescue us from God's coming judgment (v. 10b).

Therefore, turn to the living and true God by believing in his Son (v. 9).

As in Athens, the content of Paul's preaching is more theocentric than Christocentric, since he must call gentiles to turn from the worship of idols to faith in the living and true God of Israel.

After this initial proclamation about the living and true God, Paul introduces the kerygma about Jesus, the Son of God, whom the living and true God raised from the dead to bring people to salvation and deliver them from the coming judgment.

The Truth of the Gospel (Galatians)

In his letter to the Galatians, Paul makes several references to the gospel he was entrusted to preach. The letter is polemical in tone because other evangelists have come to Galatia and disturbed the Galatians. They are criticizing the gospel Paul proclaimed, claiming it was inadequate because it did not require the Galatians to be circumcised and to follow the prescriptions of the Mosaic law. Accordingly, Paul must assure the congregation he planted of the truth of the gospel (Gal. 2:5, 14) that he proclaimed to them.

The truth of the gospel that Paul first proclaimed to the Galatians called them to believe in Jesus Christ, whom Paul had vividly portrayed as crucified. Consequently, in his letter he cries, "You foolish Galatians! Who has bewitched you? It was before your eyes that Jesus Christ was publicly exhibited as crucified!" (3:1).

The evangelists who have come to Galatia have been very persuasive, and at the outset of the letter Paul laments that the Galatians are turning to a different gospel (1:6), a perversion of the gospel about the crucified Christ that he preached (1:7). By insisting on circumcision and legal observance, these evangelists have called into question the sufficiency of what God did in Christ.[12]

In the face of this crisis, Paul recalls the central event of his life, his call and conversion, in order to assure the Galatians that the gospel he preaches to them is not of human origin, nor was it something he was taught by others. It was given to him "through

---

12. If the Galatians and other gentiles had to be circumcised and follow all the prescriptions of the Jewish law, why did God send his Son into the world? Why not just ask gentiles to become observant Jews? The fact that God sent his Son into the world implies that God had done something new in Christ that the law and circumcision could not do.

a revelation of Jesus Christ" (1:12) when God revealed his Son to Paul so that he might proclaim Jesus to the gentiles (1:16). The truth of the gospel Paul preaches is the crucified Christ whom God raised from the dead.

At the end of chapter 2, Paul draws out the soteriological implications of the truth of the gospel, which touches Jews and gentiles alike:

> We ourselves are Jews by birth and not gentile sinners, yet we know that a person is justified not by the works of the law but through the faith of Jesus Christ. And we have come to believe in Christ Jesus, so that we might be justified by the faith of Christ and not by doing the works of the law, because no one will be justified by the works of the law. (Gal. 2:15–16)[13]

It is unlikely that Paul preached justification by faith apart from doing the works of the law when he first proclaimed the gospel to the Galatians. But when other evangelists came to Galatia questioning the gospel he proclaimed, it became necessary for him to draw out the implications of the gospel for his gentile converts: namely, they have already been put in a right relationship with God ("justified") by their faith in the crucified and risen Christ whom Paul proclaimed to them. To adopt circumcision and legal observance now, as the intruding evangelists are urging, will only call into question what God has accomplished in Christ. The Galatians will therefore fall from grace (5:4).

The controversy in Galatia requires Paul to reflect on the implications of the gospel he preaches to the gentiles. And as he reflects on the gospel in the light of this controversy, it becomes clear to him that there is no need to supplement what God had done in Christ by requiring circumcision and legal observance

---

13. The updated edition of the NRSV translates *dia pisteōs Iēsou Christo* as "through the faith of Jesus Christ" and *ek pisteōs Christou* as "by the faith of Christ." The alternate (and more traditional) translations of these phrases, found in the NRSV notes, are "faith in Jesus Christ" and "faith in Christ," respectively.

in addition to faith in Christ. Jews as well as gentiles are now put in a right relationship with God on the basis of what God has done in Christ rather than on the basis of circumcision and the law.

The letter to the Galatians can be viewed as a second proclamation of the gospel brought about by the crisis in Galatia. Whereas in his initial preaching Paul called the Galatians to turn from idols "that by nature are not gods" but "weak and beggarly elemental principles" (4:8–9) and to believe in the crucified Jesus, in his letter he draws out the implications of their faith in Christ. Consequently, in addition to giving us some indication of how Paul first preached to the Galatians, this letter is an example of how Paul develops the gospel he preaches in the light of a subsequent crisis. As the Galatians hear his letter read in the worshiping assembly, therefore, they hear Paul proclaim the gospel anew. They hear a more expansive exposition of the gospel that includes a sophisticated discussion of justification by faith.

The Message of the Cross (1 Corinthians)

Paul's first letter to the Corinthians provides us with further insight into the content of the gospel Paul preached. At the outset of this letter, Paul declares that he preaches "Christ crucified" (1:23). Furthermore, he insists that he did not proclaim the gospel by means of eloquent discourse, since his primary concern was to preach "Jesus Christ and him crucified" (2:2).[14]

Paul devotes the opening chapters of 1 Corinthians to a fuller exposition of what he means by "Christ crucified" because the Corinthians have not fully appropriated the gospel he proclaimed to them. To be sure, they believed in Christ, and they were endowed with many spiritual gifts as a result of their faith. But

14. For a thorough and insightful study of Paul's preaching at Corinth, consult Duane Litfin, *Paul's Theology of Preaching: The Apostle's Challenge to the Art of Persuasion in Ancient Corinth*, rev. and exp. ed. (Downers Grove, IL: IVP Academic, 2015).

something had gone terribly wrong. They were now quarreling among themselves about the gifts they received from the Spirit, falling into factions and aligning themselves with the one who baptized them (1:10–16).

In response, Paul affirms that Christ did not send him to baptize but to preach the gospel, and "not with eloquent wisdom, so that the cross of Christ might not be emptied of its power" (1:17). This crisis, engendered by internal divisions in Corinth, becomes an occasion for Paul to preach the gospel anew to the Corinthians through this letter.

Paul finds himself in a situation similar to what he faced in Galatia. Just as it was necessary to preach the gospel anew to the Galatians through his letter, so it is necessary to preach the gospel anew to the Corinthians in the same way. He had already preached the gospel of Christ crucified to the Corinthians, but he must now draw out the full implication of that gospel for the community. The key is 1 Corinthians 1:18–25:

> For the message about the cross is foolishness to those who are perishing, but to us who are being saved it is the power of God. For it is written, "I will destroy the wisdom of the wise, and the discernment of the discerning I will thwart." Where is the one who is wise? Where is the scholar? Where is the debater of this age? Has not God made foolish the wisdom of the world? For since, in the wisdom of God, the world did not know God through wisdom, God decided, through the foolishness of the proclamation, to save those who believe. For Jews ask for signs and Greeks desire wisdom, but we proclaim Christ crucified, a stumbling block to Jews and foolishness to gentiles, but to those who are the called, both Jews and Greeks, Christ the power of God and the wisdom of God. For God's foolishness is wiser than human wisdom, and God's weakness is stronger than human strength.

Paul contrasts human and divine wisdom because the crisis in Corinth resulted from a misunderstanding of God's wisdom and power. Although the Corinthians received the powerful gift of the Spirit through Paul's initial proclamation of the gospel, they had fallen into factions that threatened the unity of the body of Christ, thereby revealing their immaturity. Because the Corinthians were in danger of reducing the gospel to worldly wisdom, Paul now preaches it anew, highlighting the message of the cross.

The gospel that Paul preaches is a message about the cross, which is foolishness to those who are perishing, but to those who are being saved, it is the power and the wisdom of God.

The gospel was received differently by different groups because, as Israel's scriptures foretold, God preordained to destroy the wisdom of the world, because in its wisdom the world did not know the living God, a theme that Paul develops in his sermon in Athens. Consequently, God determined to save the world through the foolishness of the message of the cross. This saving message, however, was rejected by Jews and gentiles alike. Whereas the former sought signs, the latter sought wisdom. But Paul has been sent to proclaim a crucified Messiah, a scandal to Jews and foolishness to gentiles. To those who have been called to salvation (both Jews and gentiles), however, the gospel of the crucified Christ is the manifestation of the power and wisdom of God.

Just as it is unlikely that Paul taught justification by faith to the Galatians the first time he preached to them, so it is unlikely that he proclaimed the message of the cross in precisely this way when he first proclaimed the gospel to the Corinthians. The new situation in Corinth, however, makes it necessary to draw out the implications of the word of the cross Paul initially proclaimed. In doing so, he says that the crucified Christ is the paradoxical revelation of the wisdom and power of God. Consequently, those who believe in the message of the cross must no longer think of wisdom and power as they once did. Since God manifests power and wisdom in the weakness and the foolishness of the cross, those who embrace the gospel must evaluate wisdom and power in a new way that is antithetical to the thinking of the world. For in Christ's death on the cross, God's power is manifested in weakness, and God's wisdom is revealed in what the world judges to be foolish.

Like the Galatians, the Corinthians heard Paul's preaching in two phases: when he first proclaimed the gospel to them and now when they hear his letter read to them in the worshiping assembly. While the essential content of the gospel Paul preached—Christ crucified and risen from the dead—remained constant, when they hear Paul's letter read to them they hear Paul preach a fuller exposition of that gospel that responds to their new situation.

The Gospel of God Is the Power of God (Romans)

At the beginning of his letter to the Romans, Paul enthusiastically greets the church in Rome, highlighting his call to be an apostle and the content of the gospel he preaches among the gentiles. As he prepares to visit Rome, Paul employs this extended greeting to introduce himself to an important community of believers who have heard about him but have not seen or heard him proclaim the gospel.

> Paul, a servant of Christ Jesus, called to be an apostle, set apart for the gospel of God, which he promised beforehand through his prophets in the holy scriptures, the gospel concerning his Son, who was descended from David according to the flesh and was declared to be Son of God with power according to the spirit of holiness by resurrection from the dead, Jesus Christ our Lord, through whom we have received grace and apostleship to bring about the obedience of faith among all the gentiles for the sake of his name, including you who are called to belong to Jesus Christ,
> To all God's beloved in Rome, who are called to be saints: Grace to you and peace from God our Father and the Lord Jesus Christ. (Rom. 1:1–7)

As in his letter to the Galatians, Paul emphasizes the connection between his apostleship and the gospel. Just as Isaiah and Jeremiah were set apart to proclaim the word of the Lord (Isa. 49:1; Jer. 1:5), so Paul was called and set apart to proclaim the gospel of God (Gal. 1:15–16). While this expression can be construed as the good news *about* God, it is more likely that its primary meaning is God's own good news about what God has accomplished in Jesus Christ.

After highlighting the relationship between his apostleship and the gospel he was commissioned to proclaim, Paul provides the Romans with a summary of "the gospel of God" (1:1). First, this gospel is grounded in Israel's sacred history inasmuch as it was already announced in the prophetic promises of Israel's scriptures, a point that Paul draws on throughout this letter, especially in Romans 9–11, where he deals with the question of God's faithfulness to Israel.[15]

Second, Paul affirms that the gospel is about God's Son, whom he identifies as Jesus Christ our Lord. In terms of his human origin ("according to the flesh," 1:3), he was a descendant of the great King David, thereby qualifying him to be the Messiah. By his resurrection from the dead, he was appointed Son of God according to the Spirit of holiness, not in the sense that he became the Son of God at the resurrection but that he was publicly declared to be God's Son at the resurrection.

After identifying the main contours of the gospel he preaches, Paul returns to the theme of his apostleship that authenticates his proclamation of the gospel. It was through Jesus Christ, the Lord, that he received the grace of apostleship for the purpose of bringing the gentiles to "the obedience of faith" (1:5), which can be understood either as the obedience that is faith or as the obedience that faith engenders.

---

15. There is no other place in the Pauline letters where scripture plays such a central role as it does in Romans 9–11. In these chapters Paul makes extensive use of scripture to demonstrate how God has always been faithful to Israel. He shows that the gospel he preaches about Christ is deeply grounded in the story of salvation revealed in Israel's scriptures.

The content of the gospel Paul preaches, then, is God's good news about Jesus Christ, the Lord, the son of David, who is the fulfillment of Israel's prophetic promises and whom God publicly declared as his Son by a powerful act of the Spirit in raising him from the dead. This gospel is the fulfillment of God's promises to Israel and now also provides gentiles with an opportunity to express their obedience to God by believing in the gospel. As in his sermon in the synagogue in Antioch, Paul highlights the intimate relationship between the gospel and the promises made to Israel. And as in his sermon in Athens, Jesus's resurrection from the dead stands at the heart of Paul's proclamation.

Because the gospel is God's gospel, the power of God is manifested in and through its proclamation. Consequently, Paul's preaching is more than the announcement of a message, as important as that message is. For when God's gospel is proclaimed, those who hear it in faith experience the power of God that leads to salvation, which Paul describes as participation in the resurrection life in Christ by which believers share through the gift of the Spirit (Rom. 8).

The proclamation of the gospel is the proclamation of God's power and righteousness, which are revealed whenever the gospel is proclaimed to those who receive it in faith. It is an act of God's power at work in the world for the sake of salvation and a revelation of God's saving righteousness revealed in Jesus Christ. The proclamation of the gospel, therefore, is not an act of rhetoric. Nor is it a matter of eloquent preaching. It is an act of God's power that reveals God's saving righteousness to those who believe.

> For I am not ashamed of the gospel; it is God's saving power for everyone who believes, for the Jew first and also for the Greek. For in it the righteousness of God is revealed through faith for faith, as it is written, "The one who is righteous will live by faith." (Rom. 1:16–17)

At the end of his letter, Paul says that he has written boldly because he proclaims God's gospel rather than his own message.

He is confident because of the grace that has been given to him "to be a minister of Christ Jesus to the gentiles in the priestly service of the gospel of God, so that the offering of the gentiles may be acceptable, sanctified by the Holy Spirit" (15:16). And now that he has completed his missionary work in the eastern part of the Mediterranean (15:22–24), he hopes to visit the Roman Christians on his way to Spain.

Before coming to Rome, though, he writes this letter to present the believers there with an exposition of the gospel he preaches. Consequently, when they listen to his letter read aloud in their worshiping assembly, they hear Paul preach to them in the voice of the one reading the letter. Romans, then, can be viewed as a sermon on the gospel that Paul preaches.

In saying that Romans can be viewed as a sermon, I am not suggesting that it was written as a sermon. Nor am I suggesting that it is the way Paul preached the gospel when he proclaimed it for the first time to those who had not heard of Christ. But I am urging that he intended it to be heard as an exposition of the gospel he preaches among the gentiles. If this is so, we can speak of Paul's epistolary preaching, the topic to which I now turn.

Paul's Epistolary Preaching

I have so far focused on a few key texts in which Paul summarizes the essential content of his preaching, which he defines as the gospel of God about Jesus, the Son, whom God raised from the dead. While this has enabled us to identify the core of what Paul proclaimed, it is not, nor is it intended to be, a complete description of Paul's preaching. To get a deeper insight into the content of his preaching we must investigate how his letters were heard. We need to discuss Paul's epistolary preaching.

Paul's letters are a different genre from his preaching. In his missionary preaching, he evangelizes those who have never heard what God had done in Christ. In his letters, he writes to those who were already evangelized to encourage, rebuke, correct, and respond to issues that have arisen in the community. Paul's letters allow him to present a fuller exposition of the gospel and what it means for their community. As the community hears his letter, Paul preaches anew in the voice of the one reading the letter to the assembly of believers. For example, when he deals with the case of an immoral man in the Corinthian community, note how Paul insists on his own presence when the letter is read: "For I, though absent in body, am present in spirit, and as if present I have already pronounced judgment in the name of the Lord Jesus on the man who has done such a thing" (1 Cor. 5:3–4). Paul's letter is a substitute for his presence.[16] When the letter is read aloud, he is in their midst and the community hears him in the voice of the reader.

Inasmuch as the community is hearing Paul encourage and admonish them through his letter, they are listening to him preach, albeit in a new way. Whereas his initial preaching called them to conversion and faith in Christ, his letters call them to a deeper understanding of the gospel. In Galatians, Paul provides the community with a fuller understanding of what God has done in the crucified Christ by his teaching on justification. In 1 Corinthians, he explains the paradoxical way in which God manifests power and wisdom in the weakness and foolishness of the cross. When we understand Paul's letters in this way, we can appreciate them as extensions and developments of his preaching.

This is not to say that Paul writes his letters as sermons; he does not. But inasmuch as he composes them to encourage and admonish the church, and inasmuch as he seeks to provide communities with a fuller understanding of the gospel, they function as sermons for those who hear them.

Romans, as we have seen, is a good case study. Paul did not evangelize the Roman community, nor had he visited it. The community

---

16. Note how Paul commands the Thessalonians to read his letter publicly in the assembly (1 Thess. 5:27). See also Col. 4:16.

has heard of him, and Paul knows a great deal about the community, as is evident from the greetings he extends to specific people in Romans 16. Before coming to Rome, therefore, he writes an extended letter that addresses questions and concerns about the circumcision-free and law-free gospel he has been preaching among the gentiles. He begins with a description of the sinfulness of the gentile and Jewish world, as seen in the light of what God has done in Christ. The entire world (Jews as well as gentiles) is under the power of sin (1:16–3:20). Next, he describes how God graciously manifested his saving righteousness in Christ, a righteousness available to all who have faith (3:21–4:25). Then he describes the new situation for justified believers. Freely justified by grace, they are reconciled to God and empowered by God's indwelling Spirit (5:1–8:39). Paul then deals with the difficult question of God's faithfulness to Israel (9:1–11:36). Last, he concludes with a series of moral exhortations intended to unite a divided community (12:1–15:13).

Listening to Paul's letter in the worshiping assembly, the Roman congregation heard an exposition of his gospel and its implications for their community. When Paul arrived in Rome, then, the Roman Christians would have already heard his gospel preached in their worshiping assembly through this letter.

While Romans is the most powerful example of epistolary preaching, other letters function in a similar way. In 1 Thessalonians 4, for example, Paul provides the community with a fuller exposition of what he means by the parousia, the return of Christ at the end of the ages. In 1 Corinthians 15, he offers an extensive teaching on the resurrection of the body. And in Ephesians he gives an exposition of the gospel comparable in depth and scope to what we find in Romans.[17] Consequently, when these letters are read aloud, Paul is preaching, albeit through the voice of the one reading the letter. Something similar happens today. When

---

17. Even if Ephesians was written by a follower of Paul in Paul's name, we are still hearing an echo of Paul's voice through this letter and its extended exposition of the salvific economy of God in Christ.

Paul's letters are read in the worshiping assembly, the assembly
of believers hears the voice of the apostle preaching across the
centuries.

Paul's Preaching and Our Preaching

In this chapter, my investigation of Paul's preaching has shown
that the content of his proclamation is the gospel of God, which
is God's good news about the death and resurrection of Jesus
Christ. It is good news for gentiles because the living and true
God is revealed in and through Christ's death and resurrection.
It is good news for Jews because the gospel is the fulfillment of
the prophetic promises found in Israel's scripture. While we do
not have a record of Paul's preaching, the manner in which Luke
portrays how he preached in Acts and what Paul says about his
preaching in his letters indicates that he focused on what God has
done in Christ. Consequently, Paul seeks to turn gentiles from
the gods they have been worshiping to the living and true God of
Israel revealed in the resurrection of Jesus from the dead. He tries
to persuade his fellow Israelites that Christ is the fulfillment of
the prophetic promises made to them. What then might we take
away from Paul's preaching?

First, the content of preaching must be the gospel of God about
Jesus Christ. Preaching is not about what we want to say on a given
Sunday. It is not about our personal interpretation of the gospel,
what interests us or touches us. It is not an opportunity to propa-
gate our politics and ideology, be it progressive or conservative, by
politicizing the gospel. It is about the cross in all of its starkness,
which remains a stumbling block for every age. It is about the
resurrection, which is as fantastical to our contemporaries as it
was to the Athenians. While it may be redundant, for those of us
entrusted to preach, the task is to proclaim the gospel, the death
and the resurrection of Christ, in a way that astonishes those who
hear it as if for the first time.

Second, our task is to unfold the significance of the gospel for the congregation. Although we have heard the proclamation of Jesus's death and resurrection, its meaning and significance is never exhausted. We must unfold the message again and again by explaining what it means to live a *cruciform life* in hope of being conformed to the risen Christ.[18] There is no single way of doing it, and the needs of one generation will differ from the needs of another. But every generation that embraces the gospel needs to enter more deeply into its meaning for their lives. Our task is to unfold its meaning, not the meaning we want to apply to the gospel but the meaning that God has already assigned to the gospel. Such a task requires intimacy with and reverence for the scriptures and a deep knowledge of the church's tradition. It is a lifelong task that is life-changing for us who seek to be faithful to our ministry of preaching.

Third, the task of preaching requires those of us who proclaim the word to undertake a new evangelization.[19] A new evangelization requires us to confront cultural Christianity, by which I mean a Christianity that has not had a personal encounter with the crucified and risen Christ. The push for a new evangelization requires us to present the gospel of God in a way that leads longtime Christians to embrace their faith anew, as if they were hearing the summons of the gospel for the first time.

Consider how many Christians come to church week after week but whose lives are not touched by the power of Christ's death and resurrection. They have heard the gospel, but they have not embraced it as a way of life that makes a total claim on them. The work of proclaiming the word can be daunting. Like Paul, we must find a way to preach the gospel so that our congregations will hear it as if for the first time. We must evangelize our congregations anew.

18. This is a term made popular by Michael Gorman, *Cruciformity: Paul's Narrative Spirituality of the Cross*, 20th anniv. ed. (Grand Rapids: Eerdmans, 2021).
19. On the topic of a new evangelization, see Ronald D. Witherup, *Saint Paul and the New Evangelization* (Collegeville, MN: Liturgical Press, 2013).

3

How Paul Preached

My speech and my proclamation were made
not with persuasive words of wisdom.

—1 Corinthians 2:4

In the previous two chapters, I examined *why* and *what* Paul
preached. I noted the close relationship between these two questions inasmuch as the content of what Paul proclaimed was given
to him when the risen Christ commissioned him to preach the
gospel. *What* he preached was grounded in *why* he preached. In
this chapter, I take up a third question: *how* did Paul preach the
gospel he was sent to proclaim? We shall see that just as Paul's
commission to proclaim the gospel determined the content of
what he preached, so the content of his preaching determined *how*
he proclaimed the gospel. These three questions are intimately
related to one another.

Why did Paul preach?

Because he was commissioned to preach . . .

What did Paul preach?

the gospel he received when he was commissioned to preach . . .

How did Paul preach?

in a way that modeled the *gospel* he was commissioned to preach.

In asking how Paul preached, I am not so much concerned with the style or rhetoric of his speech as with how he envisioned his preaching, a question that we who proclaim the gospel ought to ask ourselves. Should we try to persuade others by our rhetorical skill, by our wisdom, by our theological acumen, by our insight into the human condition? The list goes on. As we shall see, how Paul preached was defined by the gospel of the crucified Christ that he received. To explain what I mean, I deal with three issues in this chapter: (1) why some in Corinth criticized how Paul proclaimed the gospel, (2) Paul's description of his preaching in Corinth, and (3) the integrity with which Paul preached the gospel to the Thessalonians.

Not a Trained Speaker

No preacher is without critics, Paul included! This is nowhere more apparent than in 2 Corinthians, an epistle that is deeply personal, surprisingly polemical, and profoundly theological. In this letter Paul defends his preaching because other evangelists, whom he calls "super-apostles," have come to Corinth and intruded on the missionary field that had been assigned to him.[1] These evangelists were, in the eyes of the Corinthians, attractive ministers

---

1. Paul's polemic against the "super-apostles" is found in 2 Corinthians 10–13. While we do not know who they were, they appear to be evangelists who came to Corinth after Paul had already evangelized the Corinthians. Paul may well have been the one who coined the term "super-apostles," which he employs with sarcasm to highlight their self-boasting.

of the gospel because they preached with rhetorical skill. In comparison to them, Paul appears as a weak and inferior apostle who lacks their power and oratorical skill. Faced with this criticism, Paul must defend himself by explaining where the power of his ministry resides. He must defend *how* he proclaimed the gospel to the Corinthians.

The crucial issue is the difference between Paul and the super-apostles. Whereas they are eloquent preachers, Paul is not, at least not in his own estimation. Paul is aware of this criticism and knows that some of the Corinthians are chiding him for the dissonance between the powerful letters he writes and the weakness of his bodily presence when in their midst. When the Corinthians listen to his letters, Paul appears powerful and intimidating, but when he is present, the quality of his speech does not match his powerful letters. Paul acknowledges this criticism:

> For someone says, "His letters are weighty and strong, but his bodily presence is weak and his speech contemptible." Let such a person understand that what we say by letter when absent we will also do when present. (2 Cor. 10:10–11)

Paul even concedes that he is not a trained orator. But that does not mean he is inferior to the super-apostles who have come to Corinth boasting of their ministerial achievements:

> I think that I am not in the least inferior to these super-apostles. Even if I am untrained in speech, I certainly am not with respect to knowledge; certainly in every way and in all things we have made this evident to you. (2 Cor. 11:5–6)

Whereas the Corinthians identify the difference between Paul and the super-apostles in terms of rhetoric, Paul identifies it in terms of boasting. The super-apostles boast of their ministerial achievements; Paul boasts of his weakness, which identifies him with the crucified Christ whom he preaches.

. . . since you desire proof that Christ is speaking in me. He is not
weak in dealing with you but is powerful in you. For he was crucified in weakness but lives by the power of God. For we are weak
in him, but in dealing with you we will live with him by the power
of God. (2 Cor. 13:3–4)

The super-apostles preach the gospel with powerful rhetoric
that is pleasing to the Corinthians. Paul preaches in a way that
mirrors the weakness of the crucified Christ he proclaims. The
super-apostles boast in their ministerial achievements; Paul boasts
in what Christ has worked through him because he knows that
Christ, who was manifested in weakness on the cross, now lives
by the power of God. Accordingly, Paul joyfully embraces the
weaknesses and shortcomings of his ministry in order to mirror
and proclaim the weakness of the cross on which God chose to
display his power.

Rather than proclaim the gospel as a skilled orator, Paul
preaches in a way that manifests the meekness and gentleness of
Christ:

I myself, Paul, appeal to you by the meekness and gentleness of
Christ—I who am humble when face to face with you but bold
toward you when I am away!— I ask that when I am present I need
not show boldness by daring to oppose those who think we are
acting according to human standards. (2 Cor. 10:1–2)

The power of Paul's preaching does not reside in his skill as
an orator but in the power of the gospel. It is the power of the
word of the gospel, not the power of his words, that overcomes
the arguments of his opponents:

For the weapons of our warfare are not merely human, but they
have divine power to destroy strongholds. We destroy arguments
and every proud obstacle raised up against the knowledge of God,
and we take every thought captive to obey Christ. (2 Cor. 10:4–5)

Here is an initial answer to *how* Paul preached: When Paul preaches, he seeks to mirror the gospel in his person so that the crucified Christ is manifested both in his life and in his preaching. He believes that those who proclaim the gospel must embody the gospel by embracing the weakness and scandal of the cross in their lives as well as in their words. Does this mean that there is no place for rhetoric in the proclamation of the gospel? Hardly! Although Paul is not a professionally trained orator, his letters show that he can write with powerful rhetoric. But in the light of the crucified Christ, Paul knows that even the most skilled rhetoric cannot manifest the crucified Christ. The weakness of the cross must be mirrored in the one who proclaims the gospel so that it can reveal the power of Christ's resurrection. Paul's most incisive argument against the super-apostles is the dissonance between their oratory and their lives, between how they preach and how they live. Their preaching, though eloquent, has led them to boast of their ministerial achievements rather than boast in the weakness and scandal of the cross. In a biting critique of them, Paul writes,

> And what I do I will also continue to do, in order to deny an opportunity to those who want an opportunity to be recognized as our equals in what they boast about. For such boasters are false apostles, deceitful workers, disguising themselves as apostles of Christ. And no wonder! Even Satan disguises himself as an angel of light. So it is not strange if his ministers also disguise themselves as ministers of righteousness. Their end will match their deeds. (2 Cor. 11:12–15)

Paul is not concerned about his lack of rhetorical skill because he has been conformed to the crucified Christ (Gal. 2:19–20). If he preaches the gospel in a rhetorically powerful way, well and good. If he does not, if his speech is "contemptible" (2 Cor. 10:10) because he is not a trained orator, well and good. The word of the gospel achieves its goal when it is preached from the cross, with the crucified Christ, from whom it derives its power. The power of the gospel itself, rather than the power of Paul's oratorical skill, determines *how* he preaches.

How did Paul preach? Paul preaches in a way that embodies the gospel he was sent to proclaim. He preaches *from the cross*, his life so conformed to the life of Christ that he can say he has been crucified with Christ (Gal. 2:19). Because he has been crucified with Christ, Paul preaches from the perspective of Christ crucified, from the cross.

Preaching from Weakness

Preaching from the cross requires Paul to embrace the weakness and shame of the cross in order to show the paradoxical way in which God manifests power and wisdom in the crucified Jesus. Paul does this in the following ways.

Paul refused to empty the word of the cross of its power. In his description of how he preached to the Corinthians, he says that he purposely did not adopt a polished oratorical style that would have been pleasing and persuasive to them lest he empty the message of the cross of its meaning.[2] Instead, he resolved to preach in a way that did not hide or obstruct the message of the cross, with all its weakness and shame. At the beginning of 1 Corinthians, he reminds those who are falling into factions that Christ did not send him to baptize but to proclaim the word of the cross, and not with eloquent wisdom lest the cross be emptied of its power (1 Cor. 1:17). He thereby offers two opposing ways of preaching the gospel: (1) preaching in a way that seeks to persuade others by one's oratorical skill and (2) preaching in a way that allows

---

2. Such a rhetorical approach has the danger of emptying the cross of its meaning by turning attention away from the scandal of the crucified Christ to the preacher's pleasing and persuasive words. If this happens, people will be persuaded by the oratorical skill of the preacher rather than by the message of the cross. Christ must be preached as crucified, as harsh and as unpleasant as this message may be. Notice how Paul describes his preaching to the Galatians: he preached in a way that Christ was publicly portrayed before their eyes as crucified (Gal. 1:1).

the power of the gospel to persuade those who hear it. From a human point of view, it would have made sense for Paul to employ eloquence and wisdom in order to persuade others to accept the gospel. But from the perspective of the gospel, it would have been a betrayal of the message of the cross.

The gospel must be presented in a way that those who hear it are persuaded by the message of the cross rather than by the rhetorical skill of the preacher.[3] Paul insists that Christ did not commission him to preach with words of human wisdom, as if the gospel needs the oratorical skill of the one who proclaims it to make it acceptable. Paul is convinced that the message of the cross, as scandalous as it is, possesses its own power that comes from the Spirit. When the gospel is faithfully proclaimed, it awakens faith through the power of the Spirit.[4] And when faith arises from the message of the cross, not from the rhetorical skill of the speaker, it is firmly grounded and cannot be shaken.

Paul does not preach with a pleasing wisdom lest his hearers embrace the gospel because of his oratorical skill and pleasing words rather than by the gospel itself. He was sent to preach a message that had been entrusted to him, and he trusts in the power of the Spirit to arouse faith in those who hear the gospel message.

Paul preached the gospel with fear and trembling. After he explains why he did not proclaim the gospel with eloquent words, Paul reminds the Corinthians how he first preached to them:

> When I came to you, brothers and sisters, I did not come proclaiming the testimony of God to you with superior speech or wisdom. For I decided to know nothing among you except Jesus Christ and

3. The message of the cross is scandalous to Paul's Jewish contemporaries because it proclaims a crucified Messiah, which is a contradiction in terms since Deut. 21:22–23 speaks of those who "hang on a tree" (an expression that in New Testament times denoted crucifixion, see Acts 5:30) as being under God's curse. Since Jesus had been crucified, it was impossible for him to be God's Messiah. But Paul insists that this is the message that must be proclaimed, as scandalous as it is.

4. In Gal. 3:1–5, Paul reminds the Galatians how they received the Spirit when they believed in the message of the crucified Messiah.

him crucified. And I came to you in weakness and in fear and in much trembling. My speech and my proclamation were made not with persuasive words of wisdom but with a demonstration of the Spirit and of power, so that your faith might rest not on human wisdom but on the power of God. (1 Cor. 2:1–5)

Paul did not proclaim the mystery of God (the gospel) with the kind of speech that comes from human wisdom and eloquence. Nor did he arrive at Corinth seeking to be accepted as wise and learned.[5] Rather than preach in a way that would have been acceptable to those who prized wisdom and eloquence, he determined that he would preach only Jesus Christ crucified, as distasteful and foolish as that message might be.

Paul reminds the Corinthians of his situation and state of mind when he first arrived at Corinth. He came to them in weakness not in strength, with fear and trembling: in weakness because he did not arrive as a powerful orator; with fear and trembling because his message about the cross had already been rejected many times, and there was no reason to suppose it would receive a better hearing at Corinth.[6] Although weakness is a matter of shame for most people, it became a badge of honor for Paul because it identified him with the weakness of the crucified Christ, thereby allowing the power of Christ to work through him.

Having acknowledged his earlier fears and apprehensions, Paul reminds the Corinthians how he proclaimed the gospel to them. He did not preach with words of wisdom in order to persuade them to believe. He did not offer them an apology for his gospel

5. Joseph A. Fitzmyer says that Paul did not come to Corinth "like the contemporary Sophists who excelled in human eloquence and gave samples of it in order to be accepted as sages in the city. He refused to provide such a display. . . . Paul wanted to be known not as a Sophist, but as a preacher of Christ crucified." Fitzmyer, *First Corinthians: A New Translation with Introduction and Commentary*, Anchor Bible 32 (New Haven: Yale University Press, 2008), 171–72.

6. The Acts of the Apostles provides many examples of Paul's preaching failing to persuade his listeners, as happened in Antioch of Pisidia (13:44–47), Thessalonica (17:4–9), and Athens (17:32–33).

of the crucified Christ. Instead, he relied on the power of the Spirit to demonstrate the truth of the gospel to them, the very Spirit who was given to them when they embraced the message of the cross. Consequently, it was the Spirit, not the eloquence of Paul's words, who persuaded the Corinthians to accept the gospel. When they did, they shared in the power of the Spirit, evidenced by the many spiritual gifts the Spirit bestowed on them.[7]

Paul insists that he preached from weakness so that the faith of the Corinthians might rest not on human wisdom but on the power of God manifested in the cross through the Spirit. Accordingly, before Paul came to Corinth, he made a crucial decision about how he would proclaim the gospel. Rather than rely on human wisdom and eloquence, he would trust in the power of God's Spirit. Rather than persuade the Corinthians by the rhetoric of his arguments, he would rely on the power of the Spirit to bring them to faith. By preaching in this way, Paul grounded the faith of his converts in the message of the gospel rather than in eloquent words.

Paul preached Christ, the wisdom of God. Paul distrusts human wisdom in his preaching because the world, in its wisdom, did not know God (1 Cor. 1:21). Thus he refuses to proclaim the gospel with the persuasive words of human wisdom. But this does not mean that his preaching is devoid of wisdom. Paul insists that he speaks a certain wisdom to those who are mature in the faith that they have embraced.[8] This wisdom, which had been hidden in a mystery from all eternity, has been revealed in Jesus Christ. If the rulers of the present age had known this mystery, they would never have crucified the king of glory, the Christ, who

---

7. In the letter opening of 1 Corinthians, Paul thanks God because the Corinthians have been gifted in every way in discourse and knowledge through the gift of the Spirit they received with the gospel (1:4–9). In chaps. 12–14 he discusses the many spiritual gifts they have received.

8. The Corinthians, however, are not yet mature in the faith they have embraced. Although they have received and believed in the message of the gospel, they have not fully understood its meaning for their community, as is evident from the divisions among them. Consequently, they did not realize the wisdom Paul imparted to them through the gospel.

is the wisdom, the righteousness, the holiness, and the power of God (1:30). Those who have believed in the gospel through the power of the Spirit, however, have received this wisdom hidden in Christ. They are spiritual people (*pneumatikoi*) because they have received the Spirit (*pneuma*) of God. As spiritual people, they enjoy the wisdom of God that is Christ.

> Yet among the mature we do speak wisdom, though it is not a wisdom of this age or of the rulers of this age, who are being destroyed. But we speak God's wisdom, a hidden mystery, which God decreed before the ages for our glory and which none of the rulers of this age understood, for if they had, they would not have crucified the Lord of glory. (1 Cor. 2:6–8)

Although Paul does not preach with the persuasive words of human wisdom, his proclamation is filled with the wisdom of God because he preaches the gospel of the crucified Christ.

How Paul preaches is determined by the gospel he was commissioned to proclaim. Inasmuch as the content of that gospel is the crucified Christ, who is the wisdom of God, Paul preaches without distracting from or removing the scandal of the cross. Rather than try to persuade others through a human wisdom that did not recognize the Lord of glory in the crucified Christ, Paul trusts in the power of the Spirit to bring others to faith. We would do well to ask what kind of wisdom informs our preaching. Do we please and persuade in a way that subtly diminishes the scandal of the cross? Do we preach with a wisdom defined by the current ethos? Such preaching, in Paul's view, reveals a lack of trust in the power of the gospel being proclaimed.

Preaching with Integrity

Perhaps the most revealing passage of *how* Paul preached occurs in 1 Thessalonians. Unlike his letters to the Galatians and the

Corinthians, in which he deals with outsiders who have come to his missionary field and opposed him, Paul writes to the Thessalonians to encourage and strengthen a community of new converts who are being harassed for their faith. Despite this harassment, the Thessalonians have remained steadfast. And so, in the opening chapters of this letter, Paul thanks God for how the Thessalonians received the gospel he preached to them and reminds them how he preached and ministered to them.

How the Thessalonians received the gospel. Paul praises the Thessalonians for their work of faith, their labor of love, and the steadfastness of their hope (1:2–3). He is convinced that they are loved and chosen by God, for when he preached the gospel, it came to them not only in word but with power from the Holy Spirit that resulted in their acceptance of the gospel (1:4–5). Having received the gospel in the face of affliction with a joy that comes from the Holy Spirit, the Thessalonians became imitators of Paul. They became a model of faith such that believers in Macedonia and Achaia were now telling Paul of the powerful way in which the Thessalonians embraced the gospel he preached to them (1:5–10). There was a Spirit-filled power in Paul's preaching that led the Thessalonians to have faith in what he proclaimed. The successful outcome of Paul's preaching among the Thessalonians was not the result of persuasive oratory but the work of God's Spirit active in Paul's proclamation of the gospel.

After reminding the Thessalonians how they embraced the gospel, Paul describes how fruitful his initial visit was among them (2:1–2), how he preached the gospel with integrity (vv. 3–9), and how he conducted himself among them (vv. 10–12).

When Paul came to Thessalonica (2:1–2). Paul came to Thessalonica from Philippi, where he had suffered and been shamefully treated.[9] Although humiliated at Philippi, he was emboldened

---

9. Luke narrates how Paul came to Philippi, where he was arrested (Acts 16:11–40), and then went to Thessalonica (17:1–9), where he preached in the synagogue but had to leave because of opposition from some of the Jewish population (17:13).

by God to proclaim the word to the Thessalonians in the face
of much opposition. Despite the many obstacles Paul faced, the
Thessalonians knew and testified that his preaching among them
was not in vain.

How Paul preached (2:3–9). After reminding the Thessalonians
of his initial visit, Paul recalls the manner in which he proclaimed
the gospel to them. The passage consists of a series of contrasting statements that show how Paul preached at Thessalonica. I
have structured the text and introduced italics to emphasize these
contrasts.

> For our appeal
> > does *not* spring from deceit *or* impure motives *or* trickery,
> > *but*, just as we have been approved by God to be entrusted with
> the message of the gospel, *even so* we speak,
> > *not* to please mortals
> > *but* to please God, who tests our hearts.
> As you know and as God is our witness,
> > we *never* came with words of flattery *or* with a pretext for greed,
> > *nor* did we seek praise from mortals, whether from you or from
> > > others,
> > though we might have made demands as apostles of Christ.
> *But* we were gentle among you, like a nurse tenderly caring for her
> own children. So deeply do we care for you that we are determined
> to share with you *not only* the gospel of God *but also* our own
> selves, because you have become very dear to us. (1 Thess. 2:3–9)

Paul begins with three negatives that rule out how he did *not*
preach. His "appeal" (proclamation of the gospel) did not origi-
nate from deceit, impure motives, or trickery. He did not act as a
charlatan taking advantage of them with flattering speech. Rather,
having been approved and entrusted by God with the gospel, he
sought to please God, who knows the heart, rather than people.
Consequently, he proclaimed the gospel in a way that was faithful
to the word entrusted to him. Aware that he was preaching God's

gospel ("the gospel of God") rather than his own message, Paul did not deceive or trick the Thessalonians in order to please them. Rather, because he had been entrusted with the gospel, he sought to please God by faithfully proclaiming the gospel of God. Paul makes three more claims to emphasize the manner in which he did *not* preach when among them. Since he sought to please God rather than human beings, he did not preach in a way that would flatter them, he did not preach for profit and gain, and he did not seek their praise even though he could have insisted on his status as an apostle of Christ. Rather, he was gentle,[10] like a mother nursing her children, because he wanted to share with them not only the gospel but his very self, since they had become so dear to him. By preaching in this way, Paul mirrored and imitated the gospel he preached.

Paul's conduct among the Thessalonians (2:10–12). In these verses Paul describes how he behaved when he was with them. First, he worked day and night as he preached so as not to burden them by requiring their support.[11] Second, his behavior was pure, upright, and blameless. Third, he treated them with the same care that a father extends to his children, encouraging them to conduct themselves in a way worthy of God, who elected and called them into his kingdom. The uprightness of Paul's conduct at Thessalonica complements the integrity of his preaching. For just as he proclaimed the gospel to them with integrity, so he lived among them in a way that mirrored the gospel he proclaimed.

Because Paul preached with such faithfulness and integrity, the Thessalonians accepted the word of the gospel, but not as a purely human word. Through the Spirit at work in Paul's preaching,

10. Some manuscripts read "as an infant." The reading adopted here ("gentle") fits the context better.

11. Paul regularly sought to support himself rather than depend on or require the support of the community. Preaching the gospel free of charge was a point of honor for him, though he did accept support from the Philippians when he was in need. The work he did to support himself afforded him opportunities to preach the gospel to those with whom he came in contact.

they understood the proclamation of the gospel as the very word of God.

> We also constantly give thanks to God for this, that when you received the word of God that you heard from us you accepted it not as a human word but as what it really is, God's word, which is also at work in you believers. (1 Thess. 2:13)

Paul insists on the integrity of his preaching because he knows that the gospel can be compromised by being proclaimed from impure motives. There are people who preach Christ from envy and rivalry and out of selfish ambition (Phil. 1:15–16). There are others who pervert the gospel by their preaching (Gal. 1:7). Others preach a different Jesus (2 Cor. 11:4) that downplays the crucified Christ. Some are mere peddlers of the word, interested in personal gain (2 Cor. 2:17), whereas Paul preaches freely, without charge (2 Cor. 11:7–11).

Although he does not identify who these other evangelists are or detail his criticism of them, it is evident from what Paul writes that *how* one preaches the gospel matters. If one preaches for profit, for gain, or for human approval, the gospel will not be proclaimed with power. If one preaches from deceitful and devious motives, the gospel will not be proclaimed with power. If one preaches with human wisdom and eloquence to cover over the scandal of the cross, the gospel will not be proclaimed with power. If one preaches without modeling the gospel in one's life, the gospel will not be proclaimed with power. For Paul, the proclamation of the gospel requires integrity of character, since those who proclaim it must model it in their lives.

Paul preached in a way that cohered with the message he received in order to mirror the gospel he was commissioned to proclaim. He preached from the weakness of the cross so that the power of God might be manifested in his proclamation. He trusted in the power of the Spirit to bring others to faith rather than trusting in the eloquent wisdom of his speech, lest he nullify the scandal of the cross. He preached with a personal integrity reflected in his conduct, and he modeled what he proclaimed. Accordingly, just as *what* Paul preached was determined by the one who sent him to preach, so *how* he preached was determined by the content of the gospel he proclaimed.

Learning from Paul How to Preach Today

How can we preach in a way that will deeply touch the lives of those who hear the word? How can we preach in a way that those who listen to the word will hear God's word through our words? How can we preach in a way that manifests a conformity between what we proclaim and who we are?

Preaching from the weakness of the cross. This study of Paul's preaching has shown that *how* Paul preached was intimately related to *what* he preached. If we hope to preach the gospel effectively today, we must proclaim it in a manner that accords with its central message: the death and resurrection of the crucified Christ. Because Paul understood this, he did not preach with the polished rhetorical style that many expected of him lest those who heard his proclamation of the gospel be persuaded by his rhetorical eloquence rather than by the message of the gospel, the message of the crucified Messiah.

Our contemporary situation is different from Paul's. The congregations to which we preach have heard and accepted the gospel. And while they may understand that a crucified Christ is a strange message, most contemporary Christians are not scandalized or taken aback by the message of the cross. The cross has become so familiar to us that we have turned it into a work of art or a piece of jewelry. Moreover, contemporary preachers are encouraged to be familiar with the basics of rhetoric because their congregations expect a well-crafted homily or sermon. So, what can we learn from Paul when he says that he preached Christ crucified without the eloquence of human wisdom?

How we preach must be guided and determined by the message we have been sent to proclaim. There needs to be a coherence between *what* we proclaim and *how* we proclaim it. For Paul, this meant preaching from the perspective of the cross, from the point of view of a crucified Messiah who died in weakness so that the power of God might be manifested in him. We who preach from the perspective of the cross and resurrection understand that the effectiveness of our preaching does not derive from our words, as eloquent as they may be, but from the power of the Spirit at work in the proclamation of the word.

Does this mean there is no room for eloquence or rhetoric in contemporary preaching? Not at all. But it is a powerful reminder that the effectiveness of the word does not depend on us who proclaim it. To the extent that the preached word is the word of the gospel, it derives its power from the message of the word and the Spirit of God at work in the proclamation of the gospel. This understanding of preaching requires us who proclaim the word to be faithful to what has been entrusted to us. It requires us to proclaim the word rather than ourselves and our personal theological views. It obliges us to be a servant of the word we proclaim rather than its master. It calls us to preach in a way that everything we proclaim centers on the message of Christ's death and resurrection.

Preaching from God's wisdom. How we preach is intimately related to the paradox of the cross in which the wisdom of God is revealed in the foolishness of the crucified Christ. How we preach should be determined by what we preach. Consequently, if our goal is to proclaim a message in tune with the spirit of the age, we will preach in a way that this age expects us to preach. Our preaching will be political; it will be ideological; it will be driven by what is current and popular. Such preaching is more common than we care to admit. Many expect this kind of preaching because it pleases and interests them. It affirms and strengthens them because it coheres with their politics or ideologies. But it is not preaching from the cross.

Paul insists that he preaches a wisdom, but it is not a wisdom this world understands. The wisdom he proclaims is the mystery of God, which is Christ, in whom are hidden all the treasures of wisdom and knowledge (Col. 2:3). It is a wisdom grounded in the cross and resurrection. It is a wisdom that cannot be understood apart from the Spirit. Nor can it be proclaimed apart from the Spirit.

When we understand preaching as a proclamation of God's wisdom in Christ, we find ourselves preaching in a different key. The purpose of our preaching is not to proclaim our wisdom but God's mysterious wisdom hidden in Christ. Preaching such wisdom requires us to preach in a way guided by the power of the Spirit of God rather than by the spirit of the age.

Preaching with integrity. Preaching requires personal integrity and transparency. To preach the death and resurrection of Jesus Christ without living a life conformed to Jesus Christ is a perversion of the gospel. We need to model and mirror the gospel we proclaim so that we can say with Paul, "Be imitators of me" (see 1 Cor. 4:16; 11:1; Phil. 3:17). Imitate me and you will know what it means to be crucified with Christ. Imitate me and you will understand the meaning of the paschal mystery of Christ's death and resurrection. Imitate me and you will be a Christian. How we preach should reflect a life lived with Christ. If preaching Christ lacks a witness to Christ, it runs the risk of becoming an academic exercise. As we preach we need to witness to the presence of Christ in our lives. We need to testify to a personal encounter with the crucified and risen one. How Paul preached demonstrated a life lived in and for Christ. How we preach will be the outcome of how we live our life in Christ.

How we live profoundly affects how we preach. If we live in and with Christ, we will preach Christ in a way that witnesses to our life in Christ. If we do not have a personal experience of life in Christ, our preaching will, in Paul's words, empty the cross of its meaning (1 Cor. 1:17). In a word, *how* we preach is intimately related to the life we live in Jesus Christ.

4

Preaching as the Ministry of a New Covenant

God . . . has made us qualified to be
ministers of a new covenant.

—2 Corinthians 3:5–6

Thus far, I have dealt with three questions: Why did Paul preach? What did Paul preach? How did Paul preach? In this chapter I turn to another question: How did Paul describe the ministry of the word he exercised within God's economy of salvation? To answer this question, I turn to 2 Corinthians 2:14–7:4, a remarkable passage in which Paul describes what he calls the ministry of a "new covenant."

Paul's second letter to the Corinthians is his most personal letter. In it he reveals his soul to a community that questioned his apostolic integrity. Paul visited Corinth on his way to Macedonia, and he had intended to visit the community a second time on his return trip. But during his first visit, someone deeply offended him, and the Corinthians did not come to his defense. Consequently, he canceled his return visit, causing some to question his integrity. To complicate the matter further, other evangelists, whom Paul dubs "super-apostles" (11:5), came to Corinth and stirred up further opposition against him. Everything that Paul had accomplished at Corinth was unraveling. In response to this crisis, Paul wrote 2 Corinthians, in which he tells his side of the story, defends his personal integrity, reprimands those who question his ministry, and urges the community to be reconciled to him. Since Paul's ministry is to proclaim the gospel, this letter, especially 2:14–7:4, provides us with a way to understand his theology of preaching. As we move through this passage, it becomes apparent that Paul presents his ministry in three ways: as the ministry of a new covenant empowered by God's Spirit (2:14–4:6), as a ministry by which he is intimately associated with the death and resurrection of the one whom he proclaims (4:7–5:10), and as a ministry that makes him an ambassador for Christ, calling people to accept the reconciliation God offers them in Christ (5:11–6:10).[1]

The Minister of a New Covenant (2 Cor. 2:14–4:6)

Paul presents himself as the minister of a new covenant empowered by the Spirit. His qualification to preach the gospel comes not from himself but from God. As the minister of a glorious new covenant, Paul in his preaching removes the "veil" that prevents people from understanding the spiritual meaning of Israel's scriptures revealed in Christ. While those who are perishing accuse Paul

---

1. The background to 2 Corinthians is more complicated than what I have said above. For a more thorough exposition of the events that occasioned this letter, see Frank J. Matera, *2 Corinthians: A Commentary*, New Testament Library (Louisville: Westminster John Knox, 2003), 1–32. Also, consult the commentaries of Victor Paul Furnish, *2 Corinthians: Translated with Introduction Notes, and Commentary*, Anchor Bible 32A (New York: Doubleday, 1984); and Margaret Thrall, *The Second Epistle to the Corinthians*, 2 vols., International Critical Commentary (Edinburgh: T&T Clark, 2004).

of preaching a gospel that is veiled and obscure, Paul refuses to falsify the gospel to please them.

Paul's Qualification to Preach (2:14–3:6)

In 2:14–3:6 Paul explains his qualification to preach the gospel. God has qualified him to preach the gospel by making him the minister of a new covenant that is empowered by the Spirit of the living God.

In the first unit (2:14–17), Paul gives two powerful metaphors. First, he portrays himself and other ministers of the gospel as prisoners who are being led in a triumphal procession by God. God has conquered Paul and, in Christ, now leads him in a triumphal victory procession for all to see.[2] But this is not a military parade in which the victor humiliates the vanquished. It is a procession that celebrates God's victory, which brought Paul to Christ. It is what Paul describes as his call and conversion. God has won over the persecutor of the church and now leads Paul in triumph, not to humiliate him but to give him a new ministry, whereby he will proclaim the one whom he once persecuted.

In the second metaphor, having been conquered by God for Christ, Paul views himself and other ministers of the gospel as the "fragrance" that comes from knowing Christ Jesus. Like the fragrance of a sweet-smelling sacrifice, he is the "aroma of Christ" that rises up to God like a pleasing sacrifice. His proclamation of the gospel, which comes from knowing Christ, is the aroma of Christ that brings some people to life and others to death. To those who have refused the proclamation of the gospel, Paul's preaching is the stench that leads to death. To those who have accepted his proclamation of the crucified Christ, his preaching is a sweet-smelling sacrifice that leads to eternal life.

---

2. Throughout this section Paul regularly uses the plural "we" when speaking of his ministry. The use of the plural suggests that others share in the new covenant ministry he describes in this passage.

Paul is utterly astounded by the power and consequences of
the ministry that God has entrusted to him in Christ: a ministry
of the word that brings death to some and life to others. Overcome by the awesome ministry entrusted to him, he asks, "Who
is qualified for these things?" (2:16). Who is qualified to proclaim
a word so powerful that it brings life to those who accept it and
death to those who reject it? Who is qualified for a ministry that
makes the one who proclaims the gospel the very aroma of Christ?
The answer to Paul's rhetorical question is "no one!" No one is
self-qualified to carry out this ministry of life and death. Those
who proclaim the word must be qualified by God.

When Paul says that "we are not peddlers of God's word like so
many" (2:17), he is speaking about his ministry of preaching. He
draws a sharp contrast between the "we" that includes him and
all who are being led in Christ's triumphal procession and those
who proclaim the gospel for profit like merchants hawking their
wares in the marketplace. He insists that authentic ministers of
the word are people of sincerity and integrity who have been sent
from God and so speak "in Christ before God" (2:17).

Since the Corinthians might accuse Paul of boasting, in a second
unit (3:1–3) he assures them that he is not commending himself.
Anticipating that some members of the community may want him
to produce letters of recommendation from other communities that
vouch for him, Paul insists that he has no need for such letters to
legitimate his preaching, for he is the father-founder of the church at
Corinth. The Corinthians themselves are his letter of recommendation that attests to what his preaching has accomplished at Corinth.
This letter, the community itself, can be seen and read by all.

In addition to identifying the Corinthians as his letter of recommendation, Paul identifies the community as a letter from Christ,
written by the Spirit of the living God. The community is Paul's
letter of recommendation, a letter of Christ that Paul has prepared
by his preaching. It is a letter written on Paul's heart for all to see.
It is written by the power of God's Spirit.

It is not an ordinary letter written with ink. His preaching is a letter that touches their hearts because it is empowered by the Spirit of the living God. Animated by the Spirit of God, it accomplishes what a merely human proclamation cannot. It transforms the hearts of the Corinthians. Here, Paul anticipates the theme of the new covenant that he will develop in the verses that follow. In doing so, he alludes to several texts in which the prophet Ezekiel looks to a day when the Lord will replace Israel's heart of stone with a heart of flesh by putting his own Spirit within the people (Ezek. 11:19–20; 18:31; 36:26–27).

In a third unit (3:4–6) Paul returns to the question he asked earlier: "Who is qualified for these things?" Who is qualified to preach Christ? Paul affirms that he is not self-qualified for this ministry; rather, his qualification comes from God, who has "made us qualified to be ministers of a new covenant, not of letter but of spirit, for the letter kills, but the Spirit gives life" (3:6).[3] With this statement, Paul alludes to the promise of the new covenant announced in Jeremiah 31:31–33.

Paul explains that God qualified him to proclaim the gospel when he revealed his Son to him and called him to preach to the gentiles. At that moment, he became the minister of a new covenant empowered by the Spirit rather than by the written code of the law. While the written code of the law revealed God's will, it could not give life. For although it made known God's law, it did not give people the inner power to fulfill God's law. In the light of his call and conversion, Paul understands that his ministry, which comes from the Spirit of the living God, is fulfilling the promises of Ezekiel and Jeremiah. His preaching is empowered by the Spirit of God who changes and transforms the hearts of those who receive it.

What Paul says about his qualification for ministry in 2:14–3:6 can be summarized in this way: Having been conquered by Christ,

3. Notice how often the noun ("qualification") and the verb ("to qualify") occur in this section: 2:16; 3:5, 6.

Paul views himself (and other apostolic ministers) as being led in
God's triumphal victory procession in Christ. In this procession,
Paul exudes the fragrance and aroma of Christ by his preaching,
which has the power to bring people to life or to death. Paul is
deeply aware that he has no competence of his own that qualifies
him for such a ministry. Whatever qualification he has comes from
God, who has qualified him to be the minister of a new covenant
empowered by the Spirit of the living God. It is this Spirit who
empowered his preaching at Corinth so that his ministry is his
letter of recommendation to the Corinthians, and the community is a letter of Christ written by the Spirit. Accordingly, Paul
understands himself as a minister of the new covenant foretold
by Jeremiah.

Preaching That Removes the Veil (3:7–18)

Having described his preaching as the ministry of a new covenant, in 3:7–18 Paul develops his presentation in two ways. First,
he draws a contrast between his new covenant ministry and the
ministry of the old covenant that Moses exercised (vv. 7–11). Second, drawing on Exodus 34:20–35, which recounts how Moses
veiled his face after being in God's presence, Paul says that his
new covenant ministry removes the veil so that those who accept
his proclamation can contemplate the glory of the Lord and be
transformed by that glory (vv. 12–18). Although both passages are
dense and difficult to comprehend, they provide us with important
insight into how Paul understands his preaching.

A comparison of two ministries (3:7–11). Paul compares the
ministry of the old covenant that Moses exercised with the ministry of the new covenant that he and other apostolic ministers
exercise through their preaching. Paul insists that both ministries
are glorious. Indeed, the ministry of the old covenant was so glorious that the Israelites could not look at the face of Moses because
it was transfigured by the glory of God with whom he spoke. As

glorious as that ministry was, however, Paul says it was a ministry of death and condemnation that was destined to be abolished. In contrast to that ministry, Paul describes the ministry of the new covenant as the ministry of the Spirit, a ministry of justification. When Paul calls the ministry of the old covenant a ministry of death and condemnation, he means that although the commandments of the Mosaic law, "chiseled in letters on stone tablets" (3:7), expressed God's will, they could not give those who heard them the power to do what they commanded, for the law was not yet written in their hearts by the Spirit, as Jeremiah and Ezekiel promised it would be. In contrast to this ministry of the old covenant, the ministry of the new covenant does provide the power of the Spirit to do God's will. It is a ministry of the Spirit that leads to justification and life.

Removing the veil (3:12–18). After drawing this bold comparison between the ministry of the old covenant and the ministry of the new covenant, Paul makes an even bolder move by comparing his ministry with the ministry of Moses. Whereas Moses placed a veil over his face so that the Israelites would not see the glory of God on his face, Paul removes the veil so that all who believe in Christ can gaze on and contemplate the glory of the Lord (Christ) who is the image of God.

To make sense of what Paul writes here, we need to recall the story of the golden calf in Exodus 32–34. After the ratification of the covenant at Mount Sinai (Exod. 24), Moses ascends the mountain for forty days where the Lord instructs him on how to construct the tabernacle. While Moses is on the mountain, however, the people persuade Aaron to make a golden calf, which they worship as the image of God. When Moses descends the mountain, he is filled with wrath at the people's apostasy, breaks the tablets of the law, and intercedes with God to forgive the people. He then ascends the mountain and receives the tablets of the law anew. When he comes down from the mountain, the skin of his face is radiant with God's glory because he has been in the presence of God. Consequently, the people are afraid to approach him. Therefore, Moses covers his face with a veil. But whenever he enters the presence of the Lord, he removes the veil, and after leaving God's presence, he puts the veil over his face until he speaks again to the Lord (Exod. 34:33–35).

Paul interprets this curious episode in the light of what God has done in Christ. Paul says that Moses veiled his face "to keep the people of Israel from gazing at the end of the glory that was being set aside" (3:13). Paul assumes that Moses knew that the glory reflected on his face would be abolished by the greater glory reflected on the face of Christ, who is the image of God. Aware of this, Moses did not want the Israelites to keep gazing intently on the glory reflected on his face because that glory was coming to an end. But the minds of the people, Paul says, were hardened, even as the minds of his contemporaries are hardened. For to this very day, when they read the old covenant, the veil is still over their minds, preventing them from understanding that the scriptures point to Christ. Rather than denigrating Moses and the old covenant, Paul accuses Moses's contemporaries of stubbornly gazing on a glory that even Moses knew was destined to end. Furthermore, he says that when his Jewish compatriots read the scriptures, that same veil prevents them from seeing the glory of God reflected on the face of Christ, who is the image of God.[4]

In contrast to Moses, who veiled his face to conceal the glory that was being abolished, Paul insists that he acts with "complete frankness." Whereas Moses veiled his face, the ministry of the new

---

4. Paul uses the word "veil" in several ways in this section. He speaks of the veil that Moses used to cover his face. He speaks of the veil that is over the minds of those who read the scriptures apart from Christ. He says that believers now gaze on the glory with unveiled faces. He also refers to the criticism of his gospel by others as veiled because it seems obtuse to them. By these references to the veil, Paul indicates that whereas the ministry of Moses veiled God's glory, Paul's ministry allows believers to gaze with unveiled faces on the glory of God in the face of Christ, who is the image of God, and so to be transformed by that glory.

covenant removes the veil, for when one turns to the Lord, the veil is removed. While "Lord" could refer to God or to Jesus, in this instance Paul appears to identify the Lord with the Spirit: "Now the Lord is the Spirit, and where the Spirit of the Lord is, there is freedom" (3:17). Consequently, believers now see the glory of the Lord and "are being transformed into the same image from one degree of glory to another, for this comes from the Lord, the Spirit" (v. 18). The image, as Paul explains in the next section, is Christ, the image of God (4:4).

To summarize, unlike the ministry of the old covenant in which the glory of God was concealed by a veil, in the ministry of the new covenant believers can gaze with unveiled faces on the glory of God reflected in the face of Christ, who is the image of God, and so be transformed from glory to glory. This lifting of the veil comes from the proclamation of the gospel, which is empowered by the Spirit of the living God. To preach, then, is to remove the veil so that those who hear the word can understand the spiritual meaning of the old covenant that points to Christ. Such preaching enables people to see God's glory in Christ and so be transformed from glory to glory.

Preaching with Integrity (4:1–6)

In this third unit, Paul returns to the theme of integrity that he introduced in the first unit, and he develops the theme of the veil that he introduced in the second unit.

First, Paul returns to the theme of his personal integrity (vv. 1–2). Aware of the mercy he received from God when he was called to be an apostle, he does not lose heart and refuses to practice his ministry with cunning, "to falsify God's word." Rather, in full disclosure of the truth, he commends himself before God for everyone to see.

Next, he develops the theme of the veil (vv. 3–4), alluding to an accusation that his own gospel is veiled or opaque, too difficult to understand. Paul replies that if his gospel is veiled to some, it is veiled to those who are perishing.[5] The god of this world has blinded such people so that they cannot see "the light of the gospel of the glory of Christ, who is the image of God" (4:4). It is not Paul's gospel that is veiled; it is the minds of those who are perishing that are veiled. Paul concludes by clarifying the content of his preaching. He preaches not himself but Jesus Christ, for the light of God has shone in his heart, revealing the "knowledge of the glory of God in the face of Christ" (4:6).

Looking back at 2:14–4:6, we can summarize what Paul says about his ministry of preaching in this way: No one is self-qualified for a ministry of preaching that has the power to lead people to life or death. Paul's qualification comes not from himself but from God, who has made him the minister of a new covenant empowered by the Spirit of the living God. The Spirit removes the veil from his preaching so that people can see the glory of God reflected in the face of Christ, who is the image of God, and be transformed from glory to glory. The goal of Paul's preaching, then, is to unveil and therefore reveal the glory of God that is Christ.

Preaching from the Death and Resurrection of Jesus (4:7–5:10)

Paul presents his preaching as the ministry of a new covenant empowered by the Spirit of the living God. His preaching enables others to gaze on the glory of Christ, who is the image of God, and so be transformed from glory to glory. His new covenant ministry, however, entails affliction and suffering as well as glory, as Paul describes in 4:7–5:10. As the minister of a new covenant, he carries the "dying of Jesus" in his body every day (4:7–15). The sufferings that come from carrying the dying of Jesus, however, are the outward signs of an inner transformation already occurring

---

5. See 2 Cor. 2:15 where he also mentions those who are perishing because they do not receive the word of the gospel.

in Paul's mortal body (4:16–18) that will be completed when he receives his resurrection body (5:1–10).

The Preacher Carries the Dying of Jesus (4:7–15)

Paul begins, "But we have this treasure in clay jars, so that it may be made clear that this extraordinary power belongs to God and does not come from us" (4:7). The treasure to which he refers is his new covenant ministry that reveals the glory of Christ, who is the image of God. The clay jars refer metaphorically to the weak and corruptible bodies of those who exercise this ministry. With these two metaphors, Paul establishes a powerful contrast between the glorious ministry he and others carry out and the weakness of their own frail human bodies, thereby acknowledging that the power of the gospel does not come from those who exercise it but from the glorious treasure they carry in their frail, mortal bodies.

As Paul and others carry out this ministry of the new covenant, they are afflicted, perplexed, persecuted, and struck down because of the message they preach, but they are not crushed, driven to despair, forsaken, or destroyed, because the power of their ministry comes from God rather than from themselves. Paul describes the afflictions and persecutions that he and others endure as carrying "the dying of Jesus" (4:10) in his body.[6] His sufferings for the gospel are a participation in the sufferings of Christ. He and those who exercise this ministry are being "handed over to death" (v. 11), just as Jesus was handed over to death. Paul's sufferings and afflictions, however, are not in vain. For when he carries the dying of Jesus in his body, the life of Jesus is made visible in his mortal flesh. And as he is handed over to death for the sake of Jesus, the life of Jesus is made visible in his mortal flesh. The result of Paul's

---

6. The unusual Greek expression *tēn nekrōsin tou Iēsou* can be construed in two ways: "the death of Jesus" or "the dying of Jesus." I have differed from the NRSVue here and taken it as "the dying of Jesus," which best expresses what Paul is saying here. He is participating in the dying of Jesus each day by the sufferings he endures for the sake of the gospel.

sufferings on behalf of the gospel is twofold. First, while death is at work in his fragile body, the life of Jesus is being made visible in his mortal flesh. Second, while death is at work in him, life is at work in those to whom he proclaims the gospel.

After showing what it means to carry the dying of Jesus in his body for the sake of the gospel, Paul quotes from Psalm 116 to explain why he remains hopeful despite the many afflictions he endures for preaching the gospel:

> But just as we have the same spirit of faith that is in accordance with scripture—"I believed, and so I spoke"—we also believe, and therefore we also speak, because we know that the one who raised Jesus will also raise us with Jesus and will present us with you in his presence. (2 Cor. 4:13–14)

In the Septuagint, which Paul follows here, the psalmist says, "I believed; therefore I spoke" (115:10 LXX).[7] But whereas the psalmist affirms that he continues to speak of the Lord in the midst of many afflictions because he believes in the Lord, Paul goes further. Paul proclaims the gospel because he believes in the resurrection of the dead. He preaches because he is confident that God, who raised Jesus from the dead, will raise him from the dead as well. Paul's preaching is driven by his faith and hope that he will attain the same resurrection life that Christ already enjoys.

What Paul says about his new covenant ministry of preaching in this unit can be summarized in this way: First, his new covenant ministry is an inexpressible treasure that Paul carries in his mortal, decaying body, thereby revealing that the power of his preaching comes from God and not from himself. Second, through the hardships he endures for the gospel, Paul carries the dying of Jesus in his mortal body so that the life of Jesus may be manifested

---

7. Albert Pietersma and Benjamin G. Wright, eds., *A New English Translation of the Septuagint: And the Other Greek Translations Traditionally Included under That Title* (Oxford: Oxford University Press, 2007).

in his flesh and in those to whom he preaches. Third, the dying of Jesus that Paul carries in his body is intimately related to the resurrection of Jesus. Consequently, his preaching is grounded in his hope of sharing in the resurrection of Jesus. Paul relates his glorious new covenant ministry to his participation in the death and resurrection of Christ. Because his proclamation of the gospel enables those who *hear* his preaching to *see* the glory of God in Christ, Paul lives in a way such that he participates in the death and resurrection of the one he proclaims.

The Present Transformation of the Preacher (4:16–18)

There is a second reason Paul does not lose heart as he preaches the gospel. In addition to his faith in the resurrection of the dead, he is aware that something is already happening to the fragile clay jar that is his body. Although his "outer nature" (the embodied self that can be seen by others) is decaying every day, his "inner nature" (the embodied self that cannot be seen) is being renewed day by day. In affirming this, Paul echoes what he said earlier: "And all of us, with unveiled faces, seeing the glory of the Lord as though reflected in a mirror, are being transformed into the same image from one degree of glory to another, for this comes from the Lord, the Spirit" (3:18). The power of resurrection is not only a future reality. It touches believers now as it transforms them from glory to glory even as their mortal bodies are decaying and wasting away.

The Final Transformation of the Preacher (5:1–10)

While Paul is aware that he is already being transformed from glory to glory, he knows that the final transformation will not occur until the resurrection of the dead. In this unit, therefore, he returns to the theme of resurrection from the dead that he introduced in his quotation from Psalm 116.

Paul describes his mortal body as an "earthly tent" that can be collapsed and destroyed at any moment. Consequently, he yearns for a resurrection body, "a building from God, a house not made with hands, eternal in the heavens" (5:1). Aware that death can destroy his fragile body at any moment, Paul is fearful of being found "unclothed"—that is, being found without a body at death.[8] And so, even now, he longs for his "heavenly dwelling"—that is, his body as it will be when it is transformed at the resurrection of the dead so that his mortal, earthly body can be swallowed up by his life-giving resurrection body.

Having expressed his desire to be clothed with a resurrection body (vv. 1–5), in verses 6–10, Paul speaks of the confidence he has because of his faith in the resurrection. At the moment, while away from the Lord, he lives by faith in what he cannot see. He strives to please the Lord, aware that all must appear before the judgment seat of Christ to give an account of what they have done. Consequently, Paul exercises his new covenant ministry with a resurrection faith that enlightens the present as well as the future. With regard to the present, he believes that he is already being transformed from glory to glory because of the power of Christ's resurrection. With regard to the future, he longs for the day that this clay vessel, this tent, will be transformed into a glorious resurrection body that cannot be destroyed.

Whereas in 2:14–4:6 Paul described his preaching in terms of a new covenant ministry that unveils the glory of God in Christ who is the image of God, in 4:7–5:10 he explains his ministry in terms of the death and resurrection of Christ. As the minister of a new covenant, Paul has conformed himself to the death and resurrection of Christ, whom he proclaims. Accordingly, he carries the dying of Jesus in his fragile, mortal body in order to reveal the life of Jesus, and he preaches with confidence because he knows

---

8. Paul is employing a mixed metaphor. He has previously spoken about his mortal body as a tent and the resurrection body as a heavenly habitation made by God. Consequently, it seems strange to speak of being clothed with a heavenly building. By employing the metaphor of being clothed, however, Paul describes how the inner self that cannot be seen needs to be clothed with an earthly or a spiritual body; otherwise the inner self will be found naked.

that he is already being transformed from glory to glory even as he waits for the resurrection of his body. To proclaim the gospel, then, means to preach from the cross in hope of resurrection from the dead.

Proclaiming God's Work in Christ (5:11–6:10)

Paul has presented himself as the minister of a new covenant empowered by the Spirit of the living God (2:14–4:6). As he proclaims the gospel, he carries "the dying of Jesus" in his body in hope of being raised with Jesus from the dead (4:7–5:10). In the following section (5:11–6:10), he explains that as the minister of a new covenant, he has been appointed as an ambassador for Christ to proclaim God's work of reconciliation and to call others to be reconciled to God, who has reconciled humanity to himself in Christ. This section has two units. In the first, Paul discusses the significance of Christ's death and presents himself as an ambassador for Christ (5:11–21). In the second, he calls the Corinthians to reconciliation and recounts his sufferings and afflictions for the gospel that he proclaims (6:1–10).

Preaching Reconciliation as Christ's Ambassador (5:11–21)

Since some have called his character into question, Paul begins with a defense of his integrity (5:11–13). He is not commending himself to the Corinthians but explaining his ministry in a way that will enable them to boast about him to those who boast about the outward appearance of their own ministry. While there are moments when he enjoys ecstatic experiences in God's presence, Paul insists that he acts rationally before the Corinthians and seeks to persuade others when he exercises his ministry.[9]

---

9. Paul may have in view the super-apostles who boast of their ecstatic experiences. If this is the case, he says that he also has had such experiences in God's

After this brief defense, Paul shows how his understanding of Christ's death undergirds his ministry (5:14–17). The "love of Christ," by which he means Christ's love for him, directs and controls his ministry. "For the love of Christ urges us on, because we are convinced that one has died for all; therefore all have died" (2 Cor. 5:14). By this powerful statement, Paul means that Christ's death on the cross involved more than Christ's own death. It touched the whole of humanity inasmuch as he was humanity's representative on the cross. He died as the new Adam for, and in the place of, sinful humanity.[10] Consequently, when Christ died, sinful humanity died with him, even though it was not aware of this.

Convinced of the representative nature of Christ's death, Paul is profoundly conscious of Christ's love for him, which impels and guides his new covenant ministry. Because Christ died for all, Paul no longer lives for himself but for Christ, "the one who for their sake died and was raised" (5:15). While some questioned Paul's integrity and accused him of boasting about himself, what he writes here reveals the depth of his integrity. As the minister of a new covenant, he no longer lives for himself but for Christ, who died and rose for him.

Paul's understanding of the representative character of Christ's death leads him to reflect on his own role as Christ's ambassador (5:18–21). He contrasts the way he once knew Christ with the way he now knows him. Formerly, before his call, he knew Christ "from a human point of view." Previously, he judged him to be a lawbreaker. But now, as a consequence of his call, he knows that in Christ God has brought about a new creation. The old has passed away, and in Christ what is new has come into being.

---

presence. But in his ministry to the Corinthians he acts in a rational way for their benefit, since recounting his ecstatic experiences would not benefit them.

10. Although Paul does not use the language of Adam here, I have introduced it on the basis of what he says in his comparison of Adam and Christ in Romans 5. Christ is the new human being who introduced grace and life into the world by his obedient death on the cross.

> All this is from God, who reconciled us to himself through Christ and has given us the ministry of reconciliation; that is, in Christ God was reconciling the world to himself, not counting their trespasses against them, and entrusting the message of reconciliation to us. (2 Cor. 5:18–19)

Paul goes on to draw out the implications of God's work in Christ. Through the representative death of Christ who died for all, God reconciled sinful humanity to himself and gave Paul the "ministry of reconciliation." As one entrusted with this ministry of reconciliation, Paul proclaims what God has accomplished in Christ for the sake of the world.

> So we are ambassadors for Christ, since God is making his appeal through us; we entreat you on behalf of Christ: be reconciled to God. For our sake God made the one who knew no sin to be sin, so that in him we might become the righteousness of God. (2 Cor. 5:20–21)

Because we who preach the gospel are Christ's ambassadors entrusted with a message of reconciliation, we dare not proclaim our own message but only what has been entrusted to us. We speak not for ourselves but for Christ. As ministers of reconciliation, we summon others to be reconciled to God by embracing God's work of salvation in Christ, who stood in the place of sinful humanity so that sinful humanity might stand before God in the righteousness of God's Son.

The upshot of what Paul writes in this rich soteriological meditation on Christ's death can be summarized this way: Those who have been qualified as ministers of a new covenant empowered by the Spirit are entrusted with a message grounded in the representative death of Christ whereby God reconciled the world to himself and brought about a new creation. Entrusted with a ministry of reconciliation, they are ambassadors for Christ who call people to be reconciled to God by embracing God's work of reconciliation in Christ.

The Integrity of Christ's Ambassador (6:1–10)

In this unit, Paul appeals to the Corinthians not to accept the grace of God in vain (6:1–3). He then provides them with a list of the afflictions and hardships he endures to show that he has not done anything to discredit his ministry (6:4–10).

Describing himself as God's coworker, Paul appeals to the Corinthians "not to accept the grace of God in vain" (6:1).[11] The Corinthians have already embraced the gospel of reconciliation that Paul preached to them. But by questioning the integrity of the one whom God appointed as an ambassador for Christ, they are in danger of forfeiting the gift of reconciliation they received. Quoting Isaiah 49:8 ("At an acceptable time I have listened to you, and on a day of salvation I have helped you") and applying it to the present situation, Paul says that now is the acceptable time, the day of salvation, for the Corinthians to be reconciled to God.

To assure the Corinthians that he has not done anything that might discredit his ministry, Paul provides them with an artfully constructed list of the hardships he has endured as Christ's ambassador. The list begins with a catalog of nine sufferings he faced "in great endurance" for the sake of his ministry: "afflictions, hardships, calamities, beatings, imprisonments, riots, labors, sleepless nights, hunger" (6:4–5). He then provides two lists, each with four items, that highlight the integrity with which he acts as Christ's apostle:

> in purity, knowledge, patience, kindness,
> holiness of spirit, genuine love, truthful speech, and the
> power of God. (vv. 6–7a)

11. The Greek (*synergountes*) does not explicitly mention God—as I have presented it by writing "God's coworker"—but this seems to be the intent of what Paul says. He and other apostolic ministers work and cooperate with God. They are God's coworkers. See 1 Cor. 3:9, where Paul writes, "For we are God's coworkers (*synergoi theou*), working together; you are God's field, God's building."

Next he uses three contrasting statements to highlight the different circumstances in which he carries out his ministry:

> with the weapons of righteousness
>> for the right hand
>> and for the left;
> in honor and dishonor,
> in ill repute and good repute. (vv. 7b–8a)

Finally he concludes with seven antitheses that contrast how he is perceived by many and how he truly lives:

> We are treated as impostors
>> and yet are true,
> as unknown
>> and yet are well known,
> as dying
>> and look—we are alive,
> as punished
>> and yet not killed,
> as sorrowful
>> yet always rejoicing,
> as poor
>> yet making many rich,
> as having nothing
>> and yet possessing everything. (vv. 8b–10)

Paul's lists here recall his earlier list of hardships (2 Cor. 4:6–12) that showed how he carries "the dying of Jesus" in his mortal body so that the life of Jesus might be manifested in him. Both lists show that authentic ministers of the gospel exercise their ministry of reconciliation by the way they live and suffer for the gospel as well as by the words they proclaim. The list of sufferings that Paul has endured for the sake of the gospel assures the Corinthians of the integrity of his ministry.

Conclusion: Preaching as Ministers of a New Covenant

Paul's defense in 2 Corinthians of his new covenant ministry is deeply personal, but he has a larger community in mind than just himself. By using the pronoun "we" throughout his argument, Paul indicates that he has other ministers of the gospel in view as well. After all, he was not the only minister of a new covenant. Nor was he the only ambassador for Christ appointed by God to call people to reconciliation. Paul describes a new covenant ministry that he shares with others and that the church exercises today. By way of conclusion, therefore, I suggest five ways in which contemporary preaching can be viewed in the light of what Paul writes in 2 Corinthians.

Qualified to preach. We regularly ask about a person's qualifications to preach the gospel. Does the preacher have the theological and oratorical skills required to stand before a congregation and effectively preach week after week? Not everyone can preach. Not everyone should preach. Preaching requires a number of skills. That said, it is important for us who proclaim the word to recognize that, despite our skills, no one is self-qualified to proclaim God's word. The word of God, which has the power to pronounce judgment and salvation, is always beyond human competency. We who understand the power of God's word recognize this. We know that we are not self-qualified to preach. Like Paul, we stand in awe of our ministry and ask, "Who is qualified for these things?" (2:16). Who is qualified to proclaim a word that leads some to life and brings others to death? Paul realized that he was qualified to preach by God who called him in Christ. It was God in Jesus Christ who sent him to proclaim the gospel of reconciliation to humanity. We who preach would do well to remind ourselves that we are not self-qualified to proclaim God's word. The ministry of preaching will always be beyond our human qualifications. We may be gifted and trained in speaking, but it is not our personal talents and training that qualify us to preach. Our qualification to proclaim the gospel comes from God in Christ. A recognition that our qualification comes from God rather than from ourselves teaches us that there will always be something in the ministry of preaching beyond our grasp and ability. It teaches us humility in the presence of the mystery of God's word.

Preaching in the power of the Spirit. We who are ministers of a new covenant acknowledge that the power of our preaching comes from the Spirit of the living God. It is the Spirit alive within us that empowers us to preach in a way that the word is heard as God's word and not as a mere human word. The role of the Spirit in preaching, however, is greatly neglected, at least in my experience. We preach week after week with hardly a thought about the role of the Spirit in our preaching and sometimes with little experience of the Spirit. A genuine renewal of preaching begins with the Spirit, who initiates renewal and brings it to fruition. We may be extraordinarily gifted speakers, theologically astute, culturally attuned to the issues of the day, but if the Spirit does not empower the proclamation of the word, the word will not be heard and received as it ought to be. The Spirit must be at work both in us who proclaim the word and in those who hear the word. Alive and present in those who proclaim the word, the Spirit enlightens and guides us to speak what God wills. Alive and present in those who hear the word, the Spirit opens minds and hearts to accept the word as God's word, even though we are weak vessels of the word. We ministers of a new covenant, then, preach in, with, and by the power of the Spirit, who qualifies us as ministers of a new covenant.

Preaching to remove the veil. In his discussion of his new covenant ministry, Paul distinguishes himself from Moses, who placed a veil over his face so that the Israelites would not gaze on a glory that was being abolished. Because Paul's ministry is empowered by the Spirit, it enables people to contemplate the glory of Christ, who is the image of God. Put another way, Paul's preaching enables those who *hear* the word to *see* the glory of God. Hearing in order to see is an intriguing way to think about preaching. The goal of preaching is to remove the veil so that others can hear and see the glory of God reflected on the face of Christ, the image of God. Preaching is a never-ending task of lifting the veil so that others may see the glory of God where they least expect to find it. It is a ministry of lifting the veil so that others can see Christ in new and powerful ways. It is a work of lifting the veil so that those who hear the gospel will be transformed by the glory of God in Christ. The preacher seeks to speak in such a way that those who *hear* the word can *see* what has been hidden for ages.

Preaching and dying with Jesus. Preaching is an embodied ministry. It is not merely a matter of proclaiming the word. It is a ministry of living the gospel we proclaim. Consequently, our preaching, if it does not reflect in our lives the word we proclaim, will be vacuous. Paul understands the role of suffering and affliction in ministry better than most, and he never tires of boasting about his sufferings and afflictions, which he describes as carrying the dying of Jesus in his body. We who preach the gospel must learn what it means to carry the dying of Jesus in our bodies so that we will be able to live and model the gospel we proclaim. I am not suggesting that we should seek suffering and affliction. There is no need for that. If we proclaim the gospel faithfully, however, we will soon discover what Paul means by carrying the dying of Jesus in his body. The dying of Jesus—the afflictions of the gospel—are the inevitable outcome of faithfully preaching the gospel. Indeed, if we have no experience of such suffering, or if our ministry is simply a matter of moving from glory to glory, from praise and acclaim to flattery and adulation, something is amiss. To preach is to carry the dying of Jesus in ourself, and to manifest the dying of Jesus is to proclaim the gospel.

Preaching the gospel of reconciliation. The goal of preaching is to proclaim what God has done in Christ. It is to announce that God was reconciling the world to himself through Christ, who took our place so that we might stand in his place before God. Reconciliation is Paul's most comprehensive metaphor for what

God accomplished in Christ. It proclaims that we are already living in God's new creation because, in Christ, God has done what we could not do: restore our broken relationship with God. Reconciliation with God is the basis for and the presupposition for reconciliation with others. We who preach have no greater task than to proclaim that the world, whether it is aware of it or not, has been reconciled to God. Preaching God's reconciling work in Christ removes the veil so that we can see the world as God's new creation. It removes the veil so that we can see the glory that is already transforming us thanks to God's gift of reconciliation in Christ.

5

Seven Theses
for Pauline Preaching

> . . . God's mystery, that is, Christ, in whom are hidden
> all the treasures of wisdom and knowledge.
>
> —Colossians 2:2–3

Having explored how Paul understands his new covenant ministry to preach the gospel of Jesus Christ, in this chapter I offer seven theses about Paul's preaching that have implications for contemporary preaching. I summarize the most important aspects of Paul's preaching in order to clarify what it means to preach in a Pauline manner—that is, from the perspective of Christ's cross and resurrection. These theses deal with the mystery of Christ, God, the Spirit, God's saving grace, our new life in Christ, the church, and the paschal mystery.

1. Pauline Preaching Proclaims Christ Jesus

My first thesis is so obvious that it can easily be overlooked: Pauline preaching proclaims Christ Jesus. The gospel of God,

God's own good news, is the gospel about God's Son, Jesus the Christ.

The content of the gospel that Paul proclaims is Jesus Christ, crucified and risen from the dead, with all that this implies for the salvation of humanity and the world. The risen one forever remains the crucified one, for the crucified one has become the risen one. This is why Paul's understanding of what God has done and is doing in Christ is determined by the death and resurrection of Christ. Likewise, his understanding of the Spirit and the community of believers, the church, is revealed in the mystery of Christ. Similarly, Paul's conviction of how believers ought to live is guided by the gospel of Christ that he proclaims. Christ always remains the content and goal of Paul's preaching because Christ is the one by whom he interprets the human condition, the history of God's people, and the purpose of God's creation.

A brief overview of some key Pauline texts shows the theologically rich ways that Paul presents Christ. Christ is the one in whom the righteousness of God is manifested, the one in whom humanity is justified, redeemed, and forgiven, the one whom God put forward as a sacrifice of atonement (Rom. 3:21–26). He is the eschatological Adam whose obedience overcomes the power of sin and death that Adam brought into the world by his disobedience (Rom. 5:12–21). He is the end—that is to say, the goal—of the law (Rom. 10:4). He is wisdom from God, righteousness, sanctification, and redemption (1 Cor. 1:30). He is the one through whom all things are and through whom we exist (1 Cor. 8:6). He is the one in whom all the promises of God are fulfilled (2 Cor. 1:20), the image of God (2 Cor. 4:4), the one who died as humanity's representative (2 Cor. 5:14–15). He is the one in whom God reconciled the world to himself (2 Cor. 5:18), the one who took humanity's place so that humanity might stand before God in righteousness (2 Cor. 5:21).

Paul composed a number of hymnic passages that celebrate the person and work of Christ.[1] The hymn of Philippians 2:6–11, for example, celebrates the obedience of the preexistent Christ who emptied and humbled himself to the point of dying a slave's death on the cross and was thereby exalted by God and given God's own name, "Lord." The hymn of Colossians 1:15–20 praises Christ as the image of the invisible God *in, through, and for whom* all things were created. He is the head of the church, which is his body, the firstborn from the dead *in, through, and for whom* all things in heaven and on earth were reconciled to God. Finally, the great benediction of Ephesians 1:3–14 sings of the economy of God's salvation as a plan "to gather up" (1:10) all things in heaven and on earth in Christ because Christ is the goal and purpose of the cosmos.

Although Paul never stopped growing in his understanding of Christ, his encounter with the risen Jesus was the defining moment when the mystery of Christ was revealed to him. The one whom he judged to be a blasphemer and lawbreaker was revealed to him as the goal and purpose of the law. The mystery of God's economy of salvation, hidden for ages, was revealed in Christ. From that moment, Paul interpreted his life and the history of God's people in and through what God had done in Jesus Christ. The crucified and risen Christ became the way in which Paul saw and understood how God was at work in the world. Consequently, his preaching is a proclamation of what God did and continues to do in Christ. His preaching proclaims Christ because in Christ he has found all the knowledge and treasures of God. Christ is the image and knowledge of God, and so Paul preaches Christ whenever he teaches, admonishes, and exhorts believers to live in a way worthy of their call.

1. Whereas Paul is the author of the hymnlike passage we find in Philippians, the hymnlike passages of Colossians and Ephesians may have originated in the Pauline circle. There are also hymnlike passages in the Pastoral Epistles that focus on the significance of Christ and his benefits that likely come from the Pauline circle as well; see 1 Tim. 2:5–6; 3:16; 2 Tim. 2:11–13; Titus 3:4–7.

Pauline preaching proclaims Christ because the mystery of Christ reveals and interprets what God is doing in the world. Consequently, we who preach the gospel are charged to interpret what is happening in the world in the light of what God has accomplished in Christ rather than interpret the gospel by what is happening in the world. Christ-centered preaching begins with a deep faith in Christ, the image of God, in whom the fullness of God dwells. It proclaims that Christ is the power and wisdom of God. Pauline preaching is never a matter of accommodating the gospel so that it will be acceptable to the world. Nor is it a matter of understanding Christ through the world, as if the world were the hermeneutical key to unlocking the mystery of God. Rather, Pauline preaching is a ministry of proclaiming Christ so that the world can see itself as God's new creation in Christ (2 Cor. 5:15; Gal. 6:15).

Paul proclaims that the power and wisdom of God are revealed in the weakness and folly of the cross (1 Cor. 1:22–25). He says he has been crucified with Christ, who now lives in him (Gal. 2:19–20). The world has been crucified to Paul, and he has been crucified to the world; that is, with and in Christ he has died to the world (6:14). By these and other striking statements, Paul shows that the cross of Christ is the hermeneutic for understanding how God is present and active in the world. Consequently, he preaches what God has done in Christ to show what God is doing in Christ. The word Paul preaches is always the gospel of Christ.

Pauline preaching is centered on the mystery of Christ, which is the mystery of the cross and resurrection, in order to reveal how God is at work in the world. We must become immersed in the life of the one we proclaim so that we can say with Paul that it is no longer we who live but Christ who lives in us, for we too have been crucified with Christ. As heralds of the gospel of Christ, we carry in our fragile bodies the dying of Jesus so that we can share in the resurrection of Jesus. Pauline preaching is rooted in an intimate knowledge and experience of the one we proclaim. Apart from such knowledge, it is impossible to preach Christ.

2. Pauline Preaching Reveals the Mystery of God

Through his preaching about Jesus Christ, Paul reveals the mystery of God in ways that he could not have imagined before his call and conversion. Prior to his call, his knowledge of God—the God of Israel—was determined by the law. The God of Abraham, Isaac, and Jacob had revealed his will in the law given to Moses at Mount Sinai. It was through the law and the prophets that Paul the Pharisee knew and understood God. But when the God of Israel revealed himself to Paul as the God and Father of Jesus Christ, Paul's understanding of the mystery of God underwent a transformation that can only be explained by the gospel about Jesus Christ.[2] Because he now knows Jesus as God's Son, his preaching about Christ proclaims the mystery of God as newly revealed in Jesus Christ. To illustrate what I mean, I turn to two passages from Romans. In the first, Paul discusses the righteousness of God in relation to gentiles and Jews (Rom. 1:16–3:31). In the second, he wrestles with the faithfulness of God to Israel in the light of Israel's failure to believe in Jesus as the Christ (Rom. 9–11).

Although the righteousness of God is a common theme in Israel's scriptures, Paul develops it afresh in the light of the gospel of Christ. In announcing the theme of his letter to the Romans, Paul affirms that he is not ashamed of the gospel. For when the gospel of God's saving justice in Jesus Christ is proclaimed, the power of God, which brings salvation to all who believe, is revealed (1:16–17).[3]

After announcing this theme, Paul explains how the gospel reveals the "wrath of God," which is God's judgment on sin

---

2. I am not implying that Paul encountered a different God in Christ. Rather, he encountered God revealed anew in Jesus Christ.

3. The righteousness of God (*dikaiosynē theou*) is a complex phrase that can be construed as either the righteousness that God confers on human beings or God's own righteousness. While scholars have defended both interpretations, the overall theme of Romans suggests that Paul has in view God's own righteousness; that is, God's justice, God's covenant loyalty.

(1:18–32).[4] Because sinful humanity refuses to acknowledge the
Creator, God is punishing humanity by allowing it to wallow in
its own sinfulness. Lest he give the impression that God's wrath
is only being revealed against gentiles, Paul affirms that the
wrath of God has also come upon the covenant people of Israel,
who are the beneficiaries of the law and circumcision (2:1–3:8).

But how can this be? Is Israel not in a more advantageous position than the gentiles, since it knows the law and enjoys circumcision, the sign of the covenant? Paul responds that despite the gifts
of the law and circumcision, all have sinned. Accordingly, Jews
as well as gentiles are under the bondage of sin from which they
cannot free themselves (3:9–20).[5]

After describing the human condition apart from the grace
of God in Jesus Christ, in 3:21–31 Paul returns to the theme of
God's righteousness to show that since all have sinned and so are
deprived of God's glory, God has freely justified all, gentile as well
as Jew, on the basis of faith in Jesus Christ.

For Paul, the righteousness and wrath of God in Romans 1–3
become, in the light of the gospel, a revelation of the justice and
righteousness of God. Whereas Paul formerly understood God's
righteousness and wrath in terms of observing or disobeying the
law, now he understands that since all were under the power of
sin, God freely justifies all, Jews and gentiles alike, on the basis
of faith in Jesus Christ. God is newly revealed to Paul as the God
who justifies sinners by grace through faith in Jesus Christ, apart
from the law.[6]

---

4. While the "wrath of God" (*orgē theou*) connotes an emotion of God, it is
best understood as a way of speaking of God's just judgment on sin. Judgment
plays a central role in Paul's theology. See Brendan Byrne, *Paul and the Economy
of Salvation: Reading from the Perspective of the Last Judgment* (Grand Rapids:
Baker Academic, 2021).

5. Later, in Rom. 5:12–21, Paul explains how this situation of universal sinfulness came about through the sin of Adam, which all have ratified by their own sins.

6. Paul is not denigrating the law. In the light of Christ, however, he now understands that the law could not bring about justification, nor was that its purpose. Its
purpose, in God's plan, was achieved in Christ (Rom. 10:4).

That God justifies sinners on the basis of faith rather than on the basis of legal observance raises a question about the faithfulness of God to Israel: What was the purpose of the law then? Has God been unfaithful to Israel? Has God rejected his people? These are the theological issues Paul addresses in Romans 9–11.

Paul insists that the word of God has not failed (Rom. 9:6), and he is adamant that God's ways have not changed. God has not rejected his people (11:1). Israel remains the covenant people, for the gifts and call of God are irrevocable, and in God's time all Israel will be saved (11:26). But in the light of Christ, Paul now understands how God has been acting in Christ for both gentiles and Jews. First, God has always acted on the basis of election and continues to do so as gentiles are being brought into the people of Israel (9:6–18). Second, the righteousness that comes from God, which gentiles now enjoy, is the outcome of faith in Christ rather than works of the law, since Christ is the end—the goal—of the law (10:4). Finally, the failure of Israel is part of a mysterious plan to bring the gentiles to faith. The coming of the gentiles to faith, however, is not the conclusion of the story. For just as the failure of Israel brought the gentiles to faith, so their faith will bring Israel to faith, for the gifts and call of God are irrevocable. Overcome by the generous righteousness of God revealed in Jesus Christ to both gentile and Jew, Paul writes,

O the depth of the riches and wisdom and knowledge of God!
How unsearchable are his judgments and how inscrutable his ways!

"For who has known the mind of the Lord?
    Or who has been his counselor?"
"Or who has given a gift to him,
    to receive a gift in return?"

For from him and through him and to him are all things. To him be the glory forever. Amen. (Rom. 11:33–36)

The upshot of what Paul proclaims in Romans 1–3 and 9–11 is this: the proclamation of the gospel about Jesus Christ reveals God anew. God is always just and true. God has elected and chosen whom he wills. But the meaning of God's righteousness and wrath, and how God acts with those he elects, has been revealed anew in Jesus Christ. God reveals his righteousness and judgment in and through faith in Jesus Christ. God shows faithfulness and covenant loyalty through Jesus Christ. To know Jesus Christ is to know God as righteous and faithful. The God of Israel has not changed, for the God of Israel is the God and Father of Jesus Christ. In Jesus Christ, however, the God of Israel has been revealed in new and surprising ways.

Pauline preaching brings people to a fuller understanding of how God acts in their lives and in the world through Jesus Christ. It shows that God's faithfulness and justice are for all, not just a chosen few. It summons people to know God through trusting faith in Christ. While something of God can be known from creation, as Paul affirms in Romans 1:19–20, the righteousness of God is revealed only in Jesus Christ. Preaching the gospel, then, is a proclamation about God, and preaching about God is a proclamation about Jesus Christ.

3. Pauline Preaching Is Empowered by the Spirit

Paul is a minister of the new covenant empowered by the Spirit of the living God. Consequently, he proclaims the gospel through the power of God's Spirit at work in him. Likewise, when the gospel is preached, it is the power of the Spirit that enables those who hear it to comprehend and believe what is being proclaimed. The power and effectiveness of Paul's preaching, therefore, comes from the Spirit rather than from himself.

Paul is deeply aware of the power of the Spirit in his preaching, as the following three passages show:

> For I will not be so bold as to speak of anything except what Christ has accomplished through me to win obedience from the gentiles,

by word and deed, by the power of signs and wonders, *by the power of the Spirit*, so that from Jerusalem and as far around as Illyricum I have fully proclaimed the gospel of Christ. (Rom. 15:18 19)

My speech and my proclamation were made not with persuasive words of wisdom *but with a demonstration of the Spirit and of power.* (1 Cor. 2:4)

Our message of the gospel came to you not in word only but also *in power and in the Holy Spirit and with full conviction*; just as you know what kind of persons we proved to be among you for your sake. (1 Thess. 1:5)[7]

Although Paul acknowledges that he did not preach the gospel to the Corinthians with the persuasive words of wisdom they expected (1 Cor. 2:1–5), he insists that he does speak a mysterious, hidden wisdom to those who are mature in faith.[8] This mysterious, hidden wisdom is the gospel of the crucified Christ, which is revealed through the Spirit (2:6–10). Drawing an analogy between the human spirit and the Spirit of God, Paul says that just as it is only the human spirit that knows what pertains to the inner self, so it is only the Spirit of God who knows what pertains to God (2:11). Then, he boldly insists that he has received the Spirit of God so that he might understand what pertains to God. Consequently, when he preaches and teaches the gospel, he does so in words taught by the Spirit (2:12–13).

Having spoken of himself as one who has the gift of the Spirit when he preaches and teaches, Paul turns his attention to those

---

7. In other texts, Paul insists it is the power of God or Christ that is at work in his ministry. In 2 Cor. 4:7 he writes, "But we have this treasure in clay jars, so that it may be made clear that this extraordinary power belongs to God and does not come from us." And in 2 Cor. 12:9 he writes, "But he said to me, 'My grace is sufficient for you, for power is made perfect in weakness.' So I will boast all the more gladly of my weaknesses, so that the power of Christ may dwell in me."

8. Those who are "mature" (*teleioi*) are "spiritual" (*pneumatikoi*) because they have the gift of the Spirit.

who hear the gospel. On the one hand, there is the natural or "unspiritual" person who views the gospel of the crucified Jesus as foolishness because they cannot comprehend the hidden wisdom of God. On the other, there is the "spiritual" person who understands and receives the gospel because they have been given the gift of the Spirit of the living God and so have the "mind of Christ," which allows people to understand the wisdom of God revealed in the crucified Christ (1 Cor. 2:14–16).

The proclamation of the gospel is a revelation of God's mysterious, hidden wisdom in Christ crucified. We who proclaim it cannot do so apart from the power of the Spirit that reveals the mystery of Christ. And those who hear it cannot comprehend it apart from the Spirit. To preach the gospel apart from the Spirit of the living God is a fruitless task, and to try to understand the gospel apart from the power of the Spirit is likewise futile. Inasmuch as the gospel is the proclamation of God's hidden wisdom revealed in Christ, it requires the assistance of the Spirit to understand it. For the proclamation of the word to be effective, the power of the Spirit must touch both proclaimers and hearers of the word. This is why Pauline preaching is empowered by the Spirit.

4. Pauline Preaching Proclaims God's Saving Grace

Paul's preaching grew out of a profound experience of God's grace at work in his life. Even though Paul had persecuted the church of God in order to destroy it, God graciously called Paul to preach the very gospel he opposed. When Paul tells of the events surrounding his call, for example, he writes, "But when the one who had set me apart before I was born and called me through his grace was pleased to reveal his Son to me, so that I might proclaim him among the gentiles" (Gal. 1:15–16). As he looks back on his life, Paul realizes that the moment of his call, when Christ was revealed to him as God's Son, was an extraordinary moment of God's grace.

Paul always draws from that moment of unmerited grace he experienced in Christ. In the opening of his letters, he regularly extends "grace and peace" to the congregations to which he writes: "Grace to you and peace from God our Father and the Lord Jesus Christ" (1 Cor. 1:3). He employs this greeting because grace and peace (God's favor and reconciliation) are the benefits of the gospel he preaches. Like him, his converts are the recipients of God's grace and peace.

The gift of grace that Paul extends to his congregations is no ordinary gift. Whereas in the ancient world the giving of gifts was a matter of reciprocity, the gift of God's grace that Paul experienced in Jesus Christ was an unmerited gift. There is nothing he did or could have done to merit this favor. It was an unmerited gift he cannot repay, not even through a lifetime of service to the gospel. Nor was he expected to repay this gift.[9]

The grace of God that Paul experienced in Jesus Christ is the central theme of his preaching. In the simple word "grace," Paul summarizes all the benefits that God bestowed on humanity in the death and resurrection of Jesus Christ: justification, reconciliation, redemption, expiation, the forgiveness of sins, sanctification, glorification, and salvation. All the benefits of Christ are the outcome of God's unmerited favor, which is God's grace. Having received God's grace in Christ, Paul proclaims this saving grace to others. For inasmuch as the crucified and risen Christ is the content of his proclamation, the gospel that Paul proclaims is a gracious offer of salvation that God extends to all through Christ, to gentile as well as Jew.

While there are many texts that point to God's grace in Christ, here I highlight three. The first comes from a section of Romans that summarizes how all are saved by the righteousness of God as a free gift of God. The second comes from a passage of Ephesians

9. The most important work on this topic is John M. G. Barclay, *Paul and the Gift* (Grand Rapids: Eerdmans, 2015). For a more popular version of this important book see John M. G. Barclay, *Paul and the Power of Grace* (Grand Rapids: Eerdmans, 2020).

that expresses the Pauline teaching on *justification by faith* in terms of *being saved by God's grace*. The final text comes from 2 Timothy and describes the gospel of grace for which Paul was appointed as a herald, apostle, and teacher of the gospel.[10]

> But now, apart from the law, the righteousness of God has been disclosed and is attested by the Law and the Prophets, the righteousness of God through the faith of Jesus Christ for all who believe. For there is no distinction, since all have sinned and fall short of the glory of God; *they are now justified by his grace as a gift*, through the redemption that is in Christ Jesus. (Rom. 3:21–24)

> But God, who is rich in mercy, out of the great love with which he loved us even when we were dead through our trespasses, made us alive together with Christ—*by grace you have been saved*—and raised us up with him and seated us with him in the heavenly places in Christ Jesus, so that in the ages to come he might show the immeasurable riches of his grace in kindness toward us in Christ Jesus. *For by grace you have been saved* through faith, and this is not your own doing; *it is the gift of God*—not the result of works, so that no one may boast. (Eph. 2:4–9)

> Do not be ashamed, then, of the testimony about our Lord or of me his prisoner, but join with me in suffering for the gospel, in the power of God, who saved us and called us with a holy calling, not according to our works *but according to his own purpose and grace, and this grace was given to us in Christ Jesus* before the ages began, but it has now been revealed through the appearing of our Savior Jesus Christ, who abolished death and brought life and immortality to light through the gospel. For this gospel I was appointed a herald and an apostle and a teacher. (2 Tim. 1:8–11)

10. I am aware that Ephesians and 2 Timothy are letters whose Pauline authorship is disputed. My purpose, however, is to examine all the canonical Pauline letters, even if some of them may have been written in Paul's name by members of his circle.

Pauline preaching is a proclamation of God's grace because the gospel announces the gracious gift of salvation that God offers in Christ. This is why Paul is so insistent that all, Jews as well as gentiles, are justified on the basis of faith in what God has done in Christ rather than on the basis of the law or human achievement. For whatever humans can do or accomplish, they cannot reconcile themselves to God. They cannot establish peace with God. They cannot sanctify themselves. They cannot forgive their own sins. They cannot justify themselves before God. From start to finish, all is grace. Everything is the outcome of God's unmerited favor.

As I will discuss in the next section, Pauline preaching never separates the moral imperative (what we ought to do) from the indicative of salvation (what God has done for us in Jesus Christ). Rather, it calls people to live in a way pleasing to God in the light of God's grace and favor revealed in Jesus Christ. For the gospel reveals the benefits of God's grace freely given in Jesus Christ, it summons the justified to live in a new way made possible by the unmerited gift of God's grace, to live according to the Spirit.

5. Pauline Preaching Calls People to Live by the Spirit

Because God manifests his saving grace in Jesus Christ, Pauline preaching calls people to live by the power of God's Spirit. Those who are justified by faith and reconciled to God can now live in a way pleasing to God. Having been baptized into Christ's death, they are called to walk "in newness of life" (Rom. 6:4), by which Paul means "the newness of the Spirit" (7:6).

Like every good pastor, Paul regularly gives moral instruction so that his converts can live morally good lives. Even when he teaches them that no one is justified by *doing* the works of the law, he calls them to "*fulfill* the law of Christ" (Gal. 6:2).[11] Paul is

---

11. The phrase "the law of Christ" (Gal. 6:2) suggests that believers fulfill the law through the love commandment, as Christ did. See Rom. 13:8–10.

deeply aware that human beings cannot live in a way pleasing to
God by their own power. Apart from Christ, the power of sin and
the desires of the flesh are too strong, as he explains in Romans
7. If those who have been justified and reconciled are to live in a
way pleasing to God, they must draw from the power of the Spirit.
Consequently, when Paul calls believers to live a morally good life,
he does more than just tell them what to do. He summons them to
live according to the Spirit they received when they were baptized
into Christ, for it is the Spirit who empowers them to do what
they could not do formerly.

Although the Pauline letters are not to be equated with Paul's
preaching, they help us understand what and how he instructed
his congregations about the moral life, thereby providing us with
guidance for preaching.

In his letter to the Galatians, for example, Paul faces a strong
challenge to his teaching on justification by faith. If believers are
justified on the basis of faith in Christ rather than on the basis of
the law, how will they live a morally good life without the guidance of the law? In response, Paul contrasts doing the *works* of
the flesh and allowing the Spirit to produce its *fruit* in the justified
(5:16–26). Whereas the works of the flesh come from the abuse
of freedom that gratifies selfish desires, there are no works of
the Spirit. Rather, Paul speaks of the *fruit* of the Spirit brought
about in the lives of believers. The singular fruit of the Spirit is
manifested in the "love, joy, peace, patience, kindness, generosity,
faithfulness, gentleness, and self-control" that the Spirit produces
in the justified (5:22–23). The power to live the moral life derives
from the Spirit who leads, guides, and produces its fruit in those
who follow the Spirit's lead.

In Romans, Paul addresses a slightly different question. If the
power of sin, which he described in Romans 7, frustrates every
attempt to live according to the law, how can believers fulfill the
law? Paul answers this question in Romans 8, where he provides
a fuller teaching of life in the Spirit. In this chapter, he contrasts

two ways of living: according to the flesh and according to the Spirit. Those who live according to the flesh live on a purely human level. They put their hope and trust in the flesh, which is mortal and destined for death. Although the flesh is not evil in itself, it does not have the power to give life. Living according to the flesh, then, is a metaphor for a way of life destined for death.

In contrast, those who live according to the Spirit put their trust in the Spirit of God, whom they received when they were baptized into Christ. Their lives are animated and empowered by the Spirit of the living God, the promise of resurrection life. Living according to the Spirit, therefore, is a metaphor for living in a way pleasing to God. Those who live in this way fulfill the law of God, which they could not do when they were under the power of sin. The moral life is more than a matter of doing what is right. It is a process of living in the newness of life (Rom. 6:4; 7:6), made possible by the Spirit.

In saying that Pauline preaching calls people to live according to the Spirit, I am aware that letters such as Ephesians and Colossians approach the moral life in a slightly different manner. In doing so, however, they make a similar point: *the morally good life pleasing to God can be achieved only through the power of Christ.* For example, in Colossians Paul reminds the congregation:

> So if you have been raised with Christ, seek the things that are above, where Christ is, seated at the right hand of God. Set your minds on the things that are above, not on the things that are on earth, for you have died, and your life is hidden with Christ in God. When Christ who is your life is revealed, then you also will be revealed with him in glory. (Col. 3:1–4)

He then exhorts the Colossians to put to death all that is sinful and immoral in their lives (3:5–11) and to clothe themselves with virtues fitting those who belong to Christ (3:12–17). In exhorting the Colossians to live in this way, Paul is not merely telling them what to do. He is grounding the moral imperative (what they ought to do) in the indicative of salvation (they have been raised into Christ's risen life). Because of what God has done in Christ, it is possible for the Colossians to live in a way they could not live before they were raised up with Christ.[12]

These texts help us understand how Paul preaches and teaches about the moral life. Unlike a moralist who presents a philosophy for ethical living and calls everyone to live accordingly, Paul proclaims a gospel of grace that requires a new way of living made possible by the gift and power of God's Spirit.[13] Because Paul experienced the power of the Spirit in his own life, he calls his congregations to live in the newness of life in the Spirit, who empowers them to live in a way they could not live when the power of sin ruled over their lives. Freed from the dominion of sin, they can now live in newness of life thanks to the powerful Spirit of the risen Christ. Those who understand this know what it means to say that Pauline preaching calls people to live by the power of the Spirit.

6. Pauline Preaching Builds Up the Church

When Paul preached the gospel, he summoned his hearers to faith and repentance so that they might be saved from the coming judgment of God. But if those who believed and repented were to persevere in their new faith, they needed to become part of a community of faith in which their new life could be nurtured; they needed to be members of Christ's body, the church. Consequently, while the

12. In Colossians and Ephesians, Paul emphasizes the present benefits of Christ's resurrection in a powerful way. Whereas in Romans 6 Paul highlights how believers are united with the death of Christ in baptism in hope of future resurrection, Ephesians and Colossians affirm that believers are already raised up with Christ as members of the risen body of Christ.

13. Paul does, however, still make use of moral instruction. But in addition to this moral instruction, which often comes from Israel's scriptures, he presupposes that his converts have the power of the Spirit to live in a way pleasing to God. How they live testifies to whom they belong.

content and object of Pauline preaching is Jesus Christ and the benefits of his redemption, the gospel also has an ecclesial dimension
inasmuch as it seeks to build up the community of faith so that those
who are in Christ can call on the name of the Lord and be saved.

Paul's letters reveal the importance he attached to belonging to the
church. The fact that most of his letters are addressed to churches
highlights the centrality of the church for his ministry and his preaching.[14] He writes to remind the churches of the faith that he or others
proclaimed to them, to correct errors and misunderstandings, and
to build up the community of faith. In doing so, he assures believers
that they have been elected and chosen for salvation. Their community, no matter how small and seemingly insignificant, is the church
of God, the temple of God, the body of the Christ in the world.

The centrality of the church in Paul's letters suggests the important role it plays in his teaching and preaching. This is not to
say that the church is the object of faith in the way that the gospel
is; it is not. The gospel, however, cannot grow and flourish apart
from the church. Accordingly, in addition to proclaiming the gospel, Paul established churches, local manifestations of the church
of God, so that those who believe in the gospel might join with
others in calling on the name of the Lord and being saved. The
symbiotic relationship between the proclamation of the gospel
and the church can be expressed in this way:

> The proclamation of the gospel gives birth to a
> community of faith.
> The community calls on the name of the Lord.
> Those who enter this community are called to proclaim
> the gospel to others . . .
> so that they will enter the community of faith.

14. Four letters are addressed to individuals (Philemon, 1 & 2 Timothy, and Titus),
but it is clear from their content that Paul has the needs of the church in view in these
letters. He writes to Timothy and Titus to instruct them how to watch over and care
for the churches, and to Philemon so that he will act as befits the leadership role he
has in the congregation.

Paul identifies communities of faith he established as the church, the temple of God, and the body of Christ.

The church is a community of believers who have been chosen and elected by God in Christ to call on the name of the Lord and be saved. Each community is a manifestation of the church of God in a particular place. Thus, Paul addresses the Corinthians as "the church of God that is in Corinth" (1 Cor. 1:2; 2 Cor. 1:1). As members of the church, the Corinthians have been called to be the congregation of God in the world, to witness to and proclaim the gospel to others. They have been built into the temple of God because the Spirit of God dwells in them (1 Cor. 3:16–17), and so they must separate themselves from unbelievers (2 Cor. 6:14–7:1).[15] They are members of the household of God, "built upon the foundation of the apostles and prophets, with Christ Jesus himself as the cornerstone," as they grow "into a holy temple in the Lord" (Eph. 2:19–22).

Paul's most powerful image of the church is the body of Christ, which he develops in Romans and 1 Corinthians, reminding these communities that each person, with his or her particular gift, plays a vital role as a member of Christ's body (Rom. 12:4–5; 1 Cor. 12:12–17). In Colossians and Ephesians, Paul develops the image of the church as the body of Christ differently. He describes the risen, cosmic Christ as the "head" of the body, which is the church (Col. 1:18, 24; Eph. 1:22–23; 4:4–16). In Ephesians he goes further and identifies a sign of the covenant relationship between Christ and the church in the marriage covenant between husband and wife. The church is the bride of Christ, obedient to her Lord. Christ, her spouse and her head, loves her as his own body and hands himself over to death in order to sanctify and cleanse her (Eph. 5:21–33). Paul presents himself as the one who promised the church in marriage to Christ, and so he seeks to present her as "a chaste virgin to Christ" (2 Cor. 11:1–4).

15. Because they have been sanctified in Christ, the Corinthians must establish boundaries between themselves and unbelievers. It is clear from what Paul writes in 1 Cor. 5:9–10, however, that this does not mean complete isolation from the world.

The central role the church plays in Paul's letters highlights the relationship between the church and the gospel he proclaims. His purpose was to unite those who heard the gospel into a community of faith that breaks the barriers that separate Jews and gentiles. Accordingly, he proclaims the role of the church in God's economy of salvation, a plan to bring all to faith so that Jews and gentiles can become members of "the Israel of God" (Gal. 6:16).

The intimate relationship between the gospel and the church can be expressed in this way: The church is born from the proclamation of the gospel so that it can live by, be saved by, and proclaim the gospel. That Paul's converts did not always understand this relationship between gospel and church is evident from the divisions and controversies that arose in many of his congregations. As such, Paul found it necessary to preach to his congregations anew, reminding them of the implications of the gospel for their life in the church of God, the temple of the living God, the body of Christ. As he sought to build up the body of Christ, his preaching became more ecclesial. Contemporary preachers face similar challenges today, especially when the prevailing culture threatens to overcome the proclamation of the gospel. At such moments we, like Paul, need to highlight the intimate connection between preaching the gospel and building up the community of faith.

7. Pauline Preaching Proclaims the Paschal Mystery

My final thesis is the most important, since it summarizes all the others: Pauline preaching proclaims the paschal mystery.[16] "Paschal mystery" is a liturgical term that encompasses the whole career of the Christ: the mystery of his entrance into the world

---

16. Although the term "paschal mystery" does not occur in the Pauline writings, Paul does write, "For our paschal lamb, Christ, has been sacrificed" (1 Cor. 5:7), which indicates that he understands Christ's death in the light of the Passover and the slaying of the paschal lamb.

that culminates in his death, resurrection, return to the Father, the sending forth of the Spirit, and his parousia, which will inaugurate the general resurrection of the dead and God's final judgment. It is a concise way of speaking of the whole mystery of God's economy of salvation revealed in Christ.[17] This mystery, of course, is the content of the entire New Testament, indeed the whole of scripture when read in the light of Christ. Consequently, it is not limited to the Pauline epistles. Paul's letters, however, more than the Gospels and other writings of the New Testament, distinctively focus on the proclamation of Christ's saving death and life-giving resurrection. For example, whereas the Synoptic Gospels proclaim Jesus's good news about the inbreaking of the kingdom of God, and whereas the Gospel of John proclaims that Jesus is the Word incarnate, the Pauline epistles proclaim the mystery of his death and resurrection.[18]

I use the word "mystery" because the full meaning of what happened in the death and the resurrection of Jesus will always be beyond human comprehension. For even though the death of Jesus was a historical event, it was an event that transcends human understanding, since the one who died on the cross was the preexistent Son of God (Phil. 2:6–11), whose death was an atonement for sins that reconciled the world to God and inaugurated a new creation (2 Cor. 5:16–21). Likewise, even though Paul encountered the risen Christ and mentions others to whom he appeared (1 Cor. 15:5–6), the risen one had not simply returned to his former way of life. He had already entered into resurrection life, a share in God's own life. Consequently, while we can theologize about the

17. In addition to the benediction of Eph. 1:3–14, which summarizes God's redemptive plan in Christ, Paul writes, "Although I am the very least of all the saints, this grace was given to me to bring to the gentiles the news of the boundless riches of Christ and to make everyone see *what is the plan of the mystery hidden for ages in God*, who created all things" (3:8–9).

18. The Synoptic Gospels and the Gospel of John culminate in the account of Jesus's death and resurrection, but whereas the story of Jesus's ministry plays a central role in them, in the Pauline writings the story of Jesus's ministry gives way to the proclamation of his death and resurrection.

meaning of what happened at Jesus's death and the significance of his resurrection, we will never fully comprehend this singular event—the death and resurrection of Christ—until we ourselves enter in Christ's resurrection glory.

Christ's ignominious death and resurrection life reveal the whole meaning of who Christ is and what it means to believe in him. First, they most fully reveal who Christ is. He is the preexistent Son of God, the incarnate one, who dwelled in God's inaccessible glory but obediently entered into the human condition so that in him "we might become the righteousness of God" (2 Cor. 5:21). Because of the obedience of Christ, the eschatological Adam (Rom. 5:12–21), God raised, exalted, and granted him the divine name ("Lord") that is above every other name. Christ's death and resurrection for Paul includes the whole sweep of salvation history, since it is the fulfillment of the divine economy that begins with creation, continues with the election of Israel, culminates in Jesus, and will be completed with his return at the end of the ages, when all things will be put under the rule of the Son and the Son will hand over the kingdom to the Father so that God will be all in all (1 Cor. 15:20–28). Consequently, when Paul speaks about the death and resurrection of Christ, he has in view not only what happened on Good Friday and Easter Sunday but the whole sweep of salvation history that finds its fulfillment in this event.

Second, just as the paschal mystery of Christ's death and resurrection reveals the full meaning of who Christ is, so it expresses what it means for believers to live in, with, and for Christ. Believers participate in the very death and resurrection of Christ even now. Through their baptism into Christ, they share in his death and victory over the powers of sin and death (Rom. 6). Through the gift of the Spirit, they participate in his resurrection glory (Rom. 8) and are assured that if they die with Christ in this life, they will rise with him at the resurrection of the dead (2 Tim. 2:11–12). The paschal mystery of Christ's death and resurrection, then, is the pattern of the Christian life, the hermeneutic for understanding how believers live in Christ. This is why Paul says, "I want to know Christ and the power of his resurrection and the sharing of his sufferings by becoming like him in his death, if somehow I may attain the resurrection from the dead" (Phil. 3:10–11). The purpose of Paul's life, now that Christ has been revealed to him, is to know the power of his resurrection. How? By sharing in his sufferings!

The paschal mystery of Christ's death and resurrection is how Paul knows who Christ is and what God has accomplished in him. In the paschal mystery, Paul sees the whole sweep of God's redemptive economy of salvation: from creation to final judgment. He understands the deepest meaning of his life and how he ought to live in Christ. He sees the pattern for how the church should live in the world. There is no aspect of salvation that is not included in the paschal mystery.

To say that Pauline preaching proclaims the paschal mystery is to affirm that the center of Paul's preaching is the mystery of what God did in Christ on Good Friday and Easter Sunday. If we hope to share the power of Paul's preaching, we must appropriate the mystery of Christ's death and resurrection for the contemporary world. Every proclamation of the gospel, every sermon, every homily needs to be rooted in the inexhaustible mystery of Christ's saving death and resurrection. We who proclaim the gospel, who are deeply rooted in this mystery, understand that we must preach about Christ, his benefits, the new life to which he calls us, and the community of the church. For in this mystery, we find all the riches of Christ.

Conclusion

PREACHING FROM THE CROSS

I have been crucified with Christ.

—Galatians 2:19

At the beginning of this study, I asked, Does preaching matter? Is it still relevant in a digital age? Can the world get along without our preaching? As I come to the end of this book, I would like to return to that question in the light of what we have learned from Paul's preaching.

There is a certain kind of preaching that we can surely do without. We do not need more moralistic preaching that simply *tells* people what to do and then leaves them feeling guilty because they cannot do it. We do not need the kind of preaching that stokes the fires of the culture wars dividing the church, be it from the left or the right. We do not need the kind of preaching that interprets the gospel from a political stance. We do not need the kind of preaching that adapts the gospel to make it acceptable to the world. We do not need sectarian preaching that cannot see how God is working in others who are different from us. We do not need preaching that seeks to bring us salvation through human wisdom. Nor do we need self-referential preaching that trivializes the gospel with unending stories about ourselves. Such preaching doesn't matter, and we can certainly do without it.

But there is a kind of preaching that has the power to change lives. It is the kind of preaching Paul engaged in when he preached from the cross. It is the kind of preaching that begins with the realization that we are sent to proclaim a message that is not our own but has been given to us. It is the kind of peaching that is rooted in the gospel of God about Jesus Christ that will always be foreign to those who hear it unless the power of the Spirit is at work in them and in those who proclaim the gospel. It is the kind of preaching that untiringly returns to the proclamation of the gospel about Jesus Christ.

This is not to say that we simply repeat the same message each week as if there were no need to apply the gospel to the circumstances of our time. But our preaching must grow out of an ever-deeper understanding of the paschal mystery of Christ's saving death and life-giving resurrection. Such preaching reveals how this mystery is the key to understanding what God has done in the world and is doing in our lives. It is a preaching that is deeply rooted in an understanding of the word of God and the tradition of the church, by which I mean the way in which the people of God have faithfully understood, believed, lived, and proclaimed the gospel.

Just as Paul returned to the scriptures of Israel to understand what God did and was doing in Christ, so we must constantly return to the word of God to understand what God is doing now. Such understanding comes from an intimacy with the word that is the result of reading, studying, and praying over the word again and again. We always stand under the word and never above it. For it is not the preacher who interprets the word but the word that interprets the preacher. This is how Paul understood his proclamation of Christ.

Such interpretation of the word takes place within the community of faith lest it become a personal, idiosyncratic interpretation of the word. Thus, there is a need to be familiar with and intimate with the church's creeds and tradition. How has the church interpreted the word through the centuries? How have her great interpreters of the scriptures understood the word? The church's creeds and tradition provide us with guardrails that protect us from idiosyncratic interpretations that may be interesting to us and our congregations but are not faithful to the word. For just as Paul was faithful to the gospel he had been sent to proclaim, so we are called to be faithful to the word of scripture we have been sent to proclaim.

Finally, if I may return to the title of this volume, we need to learn what it means to preach from the cross, both from the perspective of the cross and from the cross itself.

We need to learn, as Paul did, how the cross reveals the power and wisdom of God so that we can see how God is still at work in the world. Preaching from the perspective of the cross means seeing and interpreting the world and the church in the light of the cross, which always points to the resurrection, just as the resurrection always points to the cross. The cross is the hermeneutic for comprehending what the gospel proclaims; it is the key to understanding our life in Christ.

In addition to preaching from the perspective of the cross, we need to preach *from the cross*. That is, we need to preach *with* the crucified Jesus. Paul understands what this means because he has been crucified with Christ (Gal. 2:19); the world has been crucified to him and he has been crucified to the world (Gal. 6:14). Through his participation in the paschal mystery, Paul knows something of Christ's crucifixion. Through the sufferings and afflictions he endures in his ministry, he experiences what it means to be crucified with Christ. Consequently, when he proclaims the gospel, he does so as one who shares in Christ's sufferings.

There is a spirituality of preaching that is deeply rooted in the paschal mystery, in the cross. When we experience something of Christ's afflictions in our pastoral ministry, we know what it means to preach from the cross. Our preaching is no longer an act of rhetoric but a proclamation born of an intimate union with Christ crucified that empowers us to speak about a mystery we cannot comprehend but in which we already participate because we preach from the cross rather than from ourselves.

For Further Study

Apart from the works of Duane Litfin and Jerome Murphy-O'Connor listed below, there are surprisingly few studies that deal specifically with Paul's theology of preaching. Despite this lacunae, one can learn a great deal about what Paul proclaimed from the many theologies of his thought that have appeared in recent years. Accordingly, my suggestions for further study primarily focus on Pauline theologies that I have found helpful.

Barclay, John M. G. *Paul and the Gift*. Grand Rapids: Eerdmans, 2015.

———. *Paul and the Power of Grace*. Grand Rapids: Eerdmans, 2020.

Dunn, James D. G. *The Theology of Paul the Apostle*. Grand Rapids: Eerdmans, 1998.

Litfin, Duane. *Paul's Theology of Preaching: The Apostle's Challenge to the Art of Persuasion in Ancient Corinth*. Rev. and exp. ed. Downers Grove, IL: IVP Academic, 2015.

Matera, Frank J. *God's Saving Grace: A Pauline Theology*. Grand Rapids: Eerdmans, 2012.

Murphy-O'Connor, Jerome. *Paul on Preaching*. New York: Sheed and Ward, 1964.

Schnelle, Udo. *Apostle Paul: His Life and Theology*. Grand Rapids: Baker Academic, 2003.

Schreiner, Thomas. *Paul, Apostle of God's Glory in Christ: A Pauline Theology*. Downers Grove, IL: InterVarsity, 2001.

Stuhlmacher, Peter. *Biblical Theology of the New Testament*. Grand Rapids: Eerdmans, 2018.

Wolter, Michael. *Paul: An Outline of His Theology*. Waco: Baylor University Press, 2014.

Wright, N. T. *Paul and the Faithfulness of God*. Christian Origins and the Question of God 4. Minneapolis: Fortress, 2013.

Scripture Index

123

Subject Index